BEATING THE ODDS: PEDAGOGY, PRAXIS AND THE LIFE-WORLD OF

FOUR AFRICAN AMERICAN MEN

by

Dr. James Oliver Richardson, Jr.

Ed. S., The University of West Florida, 2005

M.S., Troy State University, 1982

B.A., Norfolk State University, 1974

A dissertation submitted to the Department of Professional
and Community Leadership College of Professional Studies
The University of West Florida
In partial fulfillment of the requirements for the degree of
Doctor of Education

2007

Order this book online at www.trafford.com
or email orders@trafford.com

Most Trafford titles are also available at major online book retailers.

Printed in the United States of America.

ISBN: 978-1-4669-7747-1 (sc)
ISBN: 978-1-4669-7748-8 (e)

Library of Congress Control Number: 2013901111

Trafford rev. 02/27/2013

Trafford
PUBLISHING®   www.trafford.com

North America & international
toll-free: 1 888 232 4444 (USA & Canada)
phone: 250 383 6864 ♦ fax: 812 355 4082

The dissertation of Dr. James Oliver Richardson, Jr. is approved:

_____   _____
Eula M. Largue, Ed. D. , Committee Member   Date

_____   _____
 Joyce C. Nichols, Ed. D. , Committee Member   Date

_____   _____
Mary F. Rogers, Ph. D. , Committee Chair   Date

Accepted for the Division:

_____   _____
  Thomas, J. Kramer, Ph. D. , Chair   Date

Accepted for the University:

_____   _____
Richard S. Podemski, Ph. D., Dean   Date

ACKNOWLEDGMENTS

I owe my chairperson and committee members a debt of gratitude. I am especially thankful for my chairperson, Dr. Rogers, who provided guidance and spent many selfless hours providing feedback for my dissertation. Her insightful comments, high expectations and constant efforts pushed me beyond mediocrity and toward excellence. As my mentor she contributed significantly to my intellectual growth. Dr. Largue's patience and counsel supported my earliest endeavors in reaching my potential. Her deep concern for her students is worthy of emulation. I am also very thankful for Dr. Nichols' instructions and thoughtfulness early on. I owe special thanks to the participants in my study. Without their collaboration, this study could not have been experienced.

Finally, I wish to dedicate this dissertation to my wife. I really appreciate her support, patience and encouragement. Her significance cannot be calculated. I must also acknowledge my good friend and mentor Dr. Reglin.

Thank you.

TABLE OF CONTENTS

ABSTRACT

BEATING THE ODDS: PEDAGOGY, PRAXIS AND THE LIFE-WORLD OF
FOUR AFRICAN AMERICAN MEN

Dr. James Oliver Richardson, Jr.

The purpose of my qualitative research is to reveal how four African-American men overcame inferior education and Jim Crow laws. In the early twentieth century the social and economic conditions of African American men were appalling, yet they refused to accept the notion of inferior beings and second-class citizenship. Phenomenological interviews were conducted. The major conclusions that evolved from the data were that family and church were significantly important to the participants. This is a study about four African American men's pedagogy, praxis and their quest for discovery, self-realization and high expectations. My inquiry is also about their struggles, dreams, failures and disillusionment.

CHAPTER I

INTRODUCTION

I grew up in Northwest Florida during the 1940's and 1950's as an African- American male. There were several colored sections in town. Segregation was the custom and way of life back then. There were Black churches and schools as well as Black civic and social organizations. There were Black Little League baseball and Black football teams. Most young African-American males played one sport or another. At one point, there were three African-American newspapers in the Black community, and my extended family subscribed to two of them because they published stories about what was actually going on within the Black community. We never did bother to subscribe to White newspapers which went so far as to eulogize some White person about all of the good he or she had done for the Black community.

No one knew or ever figured out what good any White people were doing for us in the Black community. To my recollection, I only saw White men in my community a few times, and that was near election day to secure the Black vote. Then White men would come to the Black churches and speak from the pulpit, telling us about the good they were doing for Black people and how they were advocates for the disadvantaged. At times, they would even quote the Bible to prove that they had been called to lead Black people to the Promised Land. I loathed those times when the Black preachers introduced these white men as if they were our saviors and liberators.

Listening to the White men's hypocritical gibberish made my spirit tremble, knowing while they were speaking that I could not eat at any of their restaurants. I could not even enter the interstate bus station. Blacks were not allowed to sit down there to wait on the bus arrival. We had no choice but to wait in the baggage sections which was usually cold, dark and damp. A crowd of people would be trying to press into that small room. Black men, women and children would fall and stumble over personal belongings, luggage, and boxes. No colored person ever dared to come out of the baggage room until the third or fourth call to come to the departure area.

The first two calls were for White people. The last call was for Blacks who got on the bus and went toward the back. When White men were drunk and loud, the bus driver told them to go back with the (N….) colored folks. Even during holidays Blacks sometimes had to stand in the back of the bus when seats were available in the front. As late as 1965 Blacks were still relegated to the baggage room of the interstate bus station.

Similarly, at the city library "White only" signs adorned the front and back doors. I remember the first time I entered the White library in 1957 with my colored library card. I had never seen so many books about so many subjects. There were more magazines and books than I could ever have believed. My library experience was like going to the fairgrounds for the first time as a child.

As remarkable as my library experience was, it did not measure up to the feeling I got listening to African-American men pray in church. There was always time for God. Sunday morning church service (11:00 a. m. to 1:00 p. m.) in the Black community was profoundly meaningful. There were typically between two and twelve Black elderly men and women at the altar praying. They prayed like slaves in quest of their freedom and liberty. They prayed for a day when Black people would be treated like human beings; they prayed for the hearts and minds of White people; they prayed for their children and grandchildren; they prayed for mercy and sought forgiveness for their sins. I knew these spiritual moments authenticated that we were human beings with expectations and hopes. These moments gave us a sense of spiritual empowerment. Where else were the pedagogy of hope and pedagogy of liberation for the oppressed, the poor, and the marginalized? Perhaps they were also at work among our Black neighbors.

Back then, we grew up in a *real* neighborhood. We did not have to be close friends in order for us to be close; we were close because of our common fate. Sharing, giving and caring for each other became survival skills. Our well-being and life-world depended upon our togetherness. We were always somebody in our eyes and in the eyes of God as well. Paradoxically, we were taught to laugh and grin around White folks who were never allowed to see our scars and our self-doubts. My life-world turned out to be a place of laugher and togetherness; it was a place of liberty, self-sufficiency and hope; it was a place of safety, encircled by hatred and contempt; it was also a healing place for recovery from insults, injuries, and dehumanizing treatment. It was also a place of joyfulness since we all had our dreams of a better day despite the terrifying realities of racism. Today's African-American young men are still dreaming such dreams.

Life Without Shoes

What is life without shoes? White people may have viewed my neighbors and me as emotionally and intellectually impoverished. They were quite wrong. We were wealthy in wisdom and understanding. We were rich in family history and family gatherings. We were rich in teaching and learning from each other. We were rich in forgiving White people. We were grateful. There was love and a sense of belonging in the African-American community and a feeling of togetherness and unity. No one saw himself or herself as an individual, alone in the world fighting racism. In spite of being shut out of mainstream White America, segregated and denied educational opportunities, even in spite of being called underprivileged, disadvantaged and mentally challenged, we had a sense of dignity that fortified us against racism.

Most of us had a self-concept that thwarted negative images and stereotypes about who we were and where we came from. The Black school, the African-American community, and our families taught us that we were a new generation of hope. I was told by my family, for instance, that we were all made in the image of God. We were taught to hold on to our dreams and to use our imagination to make this world a better place. We were also taught from the old Negro spirituals that all God's children had shoes. Yet, unknowingly, I sought a

4

Black middle-class pedagogy that I thought would address racism better than the Black church.

Historically, the Black church has been an anchor for education, motivation, and autonomy. It offered spiritual hope to many persons in oppressive environments. In the Black church some American-Americans got their only feelings of hope. They met weekly to gather sufficient power, strength and assurance "to hold on and to hold out" and to go on living for another day. They were a fellowship of poor sufferers. When all seemed lost, getting on their knees and saying amen made some feel well again, at least for a short while.

Songs were often sung with the fullest possible assurances yet with mourning. These spirituals were folk songs of sovereignty and of yearning. Their focus was slavery and the prospect of emancipation. Freedom was the main idea of the spirituals, but DuBois called these *sorrows songs*. Sorrow songs articulated the slaves' history as well as present trials and tribulations. Drawing from these sorrow songs, "Perhaps no people can rise to the greatest pinnacles of ability until they have yearned and suffered and died, within" (Du Bois,1970). At some level this study explores this proposition.

Unlike the Black middle-class I expected to learn from, I came to understand that racism could not be overcome by acting White, looking White or learning about White society. With some reservations, I finally accepted my Blackness as nothing strange or different, like the fingers on my hand. Gradually, I began to construct new meanings for my life in the face of racial discrimination. Learning became a discovery process, and education became much more than mere survival or employment. It entailed a new way of thinking.

Not until I came to the University of West Florida did I realize that there was a pedagogy of hope for African-American males. To feel good about my Blackness without pretense gave me a pleasure. Learning became much more than finding a place in society or becoming somebody. It became a creative process of critical thinking and cultivating sociological imagination.

Although the Black middle-class has long emphasized academic achievement, they never lived in my neighborhood and never drank in my bar. I have never seen any Black middle-class leaders in a moonshine house, standing in the Food Stamp lines, or at the welfare window. Unlike some of my middle-class counterparts, when I look back upon Christmas, it never bothers me or any of my peers that Santa was a White man, as long as he was giving away free stuff. Polluted air and toxic water were the only other things free in my neighborhood.

Quest Narratives

From the time I left my old neighborhood I was on a journey. The story of my journey started out sounding like the chaotic, incoherent narrative of a wounded storyteller. Today my life is becoming what Frank (1995) in *The Wounded Storyteller* calls a quest narrative because I am able to make constructive meanings for my life. Quest narratives are about finding insights as chronic illness or other suffering is transformed into a pedagogy enabling the person to become someone new. In the process, of developing my quest narratives, I may be able to dispel a few myths about motivation and achievement among African-American men.

I may also disclose some common features of their life-world. In addition, my study is a place where wounded people tell their stories, and make sense of their suffering as authentic witnesses. Four African American men participating in my study are likely to share narratives about their personal suffering as well as their survival and successes. They may express their paramount values of the Black community back then, when they were coming up. Like theirs, my personal journey began growing up in a complex racial system. I smiled my way through the valleys of caricatures, prejudices and stereotypes. Cautiously, I walked through the streets paved with racial hatred and bigotry. Exiting the valley of false consciousness and self-doubt, I made my journey a quest.

I expect to find similar and common themes throughout the narratives (interview data) of the four African American participants. Perhaps I will find a postmodernist pedagogy at the core of their lived experiences. My education at The University of West Florida has enlightened me about postmodernism, pedagogy, praxis, and critical theory. These concepts promote critical thinking and transformed my perceptions about social issues while disrupting what I had taken for granted. The human mind is capable of astounding changes if a person has enough faith and conviction. But how does one change his mindset, values and attitudes?

This question has motivated me to move toward what Mills (1959) calls a sociological imagination, a new way of thinking about the intersections among social structure, history, and biography. My own evolving sociological imagination has led me to see how important it is for me and other oppressed, marginalized individuals to find sustainable meanings and purposes in a society that largely rejects Blackness. As Bulter (1998) indicates, Ralph Ellison emphasized that overcoming racism is very difficult. His novel *Indivisible Man* underscores the discrepancy between aspiration and realism. Its protagonist slowly learns that the identities he created rested on delusions. He admits that his personal identity dilemma continues even after he has begun to deal with it. Rejecting his own Blackness means repressing a great deal of his own past experiences. Disillusionment seems to be a necessary step on the journey to Black authentication (Butler).

Statement of Purpose

Overall, the African-American community has had a complex struggle in its continuing efforts to obtain equality and inclusion in American society (Zuckerman, 2000). Notwithstanding the negative impact of racial discrimination on the African American community in general and African American males in particular, a majority of African-American families now manage to avoid poverty and deprivation (Stewart, 1991; cf. Zuckerman, 2000). However, many still face oppression. Asymmetrical education and other racial inequalities did not end when Jim Crow was overturned. Whiteness is everywhere. Whiteness secured supremacy by seeming not to be anything in particular; it remains an unmarked status against which racial differences get constructed (Lipsitz, 2006).

Often overlooked in particular are the life-world and the accomplishments of African-American men. Many have been community leaders who have used their relatively advantaged position to set up organizations for uplifting the Black community. Success is not only their individual but also their collective dream. Such leaders, like the four African-American men who are focus of my study, made dreams come true (Jones, 1979; Maxwell, 1996). According to Harris (1992), Du Bois saw even such leaders' Blackness as "a life-world of always looking at one's self through the eyes of others, a world that revolves around contempt and shame" (p.149). I do not though, study these four African American men from such a modernist standpoint.

Instead, my research tilts toward postmodernism and a critical pedagogy capable of empowering Black communities. Insights about a few Black men's life-world and achievements may encourage others to adopt a critical pedagogy that will facilitate their own journeys. True learning seeks ways and means for one to participate in the transformation of one's world (Freire, 1970). How did the marginalized human beings in this study arrive where they are today? What did they know? What did they recognize? What might an educator need to recognize, as Giroux (1992) states, "in order to engage in such a struggle" (p.202)?

What did these four African-American males articulate and practice? The oppressed often internalize the likeness of the oppressor and accept his guidelines and mode of thinking. They are often fearful of taking steps toward self-determination, which requires expelling what has been internalized and replacing it with autonomy and responsibility. Independence comes by struggle, not by bequest (Freire, 1970). This struggle for psychological freedom involves

9

overcoming psychological injustice (Cose, 2002). These four African-American men may articulate or at least imply how they overcame such huge obstacles.

The purpose of my inquiry is to understand these men's life-world and lived experiences. I want to discover what sustained these African-American men through years of denial and rejection as well as inequality of education and racial discrimination. It is very important to understand not only their institutional contexts but also their pedagogy, their praxis, their survival skills and their belief systems. Maybe these African American men had dreams of living life as a human being with dignity and rights. Maybe they sought self-respect and self-worth; maybe they sought freedom. Perhaps they were seeking something higher and more valuable than money and were not necessarily striving for traditional success.

By exploring these four Black men's lived experiences, I increase my own and others' awareness about racism and its destructiveness. These men's knowledge about their environment illuminates a rigid segregated system that was abusive and oppressive. Their experiences may confirm that self-discovery and self-acceptance cannot be merely academic, but must involve serious reflection as well as effective praxis (Freire, 1970). These men's stories may illustrate an unsophisticated but crucial kind of praxis still needed today.

I want to listen to these men's stories about what it means to be a Black man in this country and how they were able to escape and rise above many hardships and achieve their goals. These individuals rose to become leaders within their community. They represent the new Negro, the mentors, the new leaders, the new Black man (Memmi, 2000). We may never know the full range of factors that propelled these men toward becoming full participants in society, but this study illuminates their experiences as fully as possible. My study thus explores how four Black men were able to put themselves on the same footing with White Americans and to achieve positions where they could choose their own destiny rather than have it chosen for them.

White and Black educators must come to appreciate that if African Americans can overcome racial oppression, including inferior housing and schooling as well as underemployment and still raise such men as these four, then they are educable to the heights of academic brilliance. African Americans of the twenty first century must be urged *to lift as we climb*. They must engage in racially significant teaching that empowers all Black students because that framework ensures the development of our democratic system (Billings, 1992).

CHAPTER II

REVIEW OF THE LITERATURE

How did African American males survive and overcome segregation? What motivated and inspired them to believe that they could do so? Before looking at the scholarly literature pertinent to these questions about the life-worlds of African-American men, I look at a person who may be an exemplar of African-American males who have overcome extraordinary obstacles and risen to great heights.

William Sander Scarborough's autobiography tells the story of a Black man born in slavery in Macon, Georgia. As a boy, he went out every day to supposedly play, but instead concealed his books and continued to break the law by learning to read, write, and otherwise pursue his studies. He was not the only African American youngster of his generation hiding his books and getting his education covertly. Frederick Douglass was taught to read in secret by his owner's wife. So was Susie King Taylor, who was born a slave in 1848 in Savannah, Georgia and learned to read and write secretly at the house of her grandmother's friend, Mrs. Woodhouse (Ronnick, 2005).

After the Civil War, Scarborough enrolled in the Macon schools, where he excelled and was no longer a secret scholar. After studying at Atlanta University,

Scarborough earned both his bachelor's and master's degrees in classics from Oberlin College and began to teach at Wilberforce University soon afterwards.

Over the course of several years, he rose to national distinction by publishing *First Lessons in Greek*, a text that made him the first member of his race to prepare a Greek textbook for university use. Scarborough contributed over 20 scholarly pieces to the official publication of the American Philological Association (APA), and became a member of the Modern Language Association (MLA) in 1883.

In January 1907, Scarborough was among those members of the joint session of the APA and the Archaeological Institute of America and he was received by President Theodore Roosevelt at the White House. In 1921, five years before his death at age 69, he represented the APA as an international delegate to a session of the Classical Association held at Cambridge University. Scarborough also served as the president of Wilberforce University and campaigned for Republican presidential candidates.

His activities brought him in contact with figures such as Warren G. Harding, John Sherman, Andrew Carnegie, James G. Blaine, and John F. Slater. Scarborough used these acquaintances to champion civil rights and liberal arts education for African-Americans. From his point of view, autonomy presupposes not only equal protection under the law but also equal access to culture and education. Scarborough openly opposed Booker T. Washington's directive for technical training. Although he held Washington in high regard, he himself remained a staunch supporter of higher learning for African Americans.

Scarborough argued that higher education is the most powerful prize in the Negro's advancement. In 1892 he was forced from his professorship at Wilberforce University in a political fight over giving priority to liberal arts education. At great financial cost to himself, he found employment at Payne Theological Seminary.

Scarborough was an eyewitness to many events. He saw Jefferson Davis led away as a prisoner of war. He heard Richard Wright call out, "Tell them we are rising!" He sat at the table with John Sherman at the first Lincoln Day Banquet held in Ohio. He saw Frederick Douglass cut a pigeon wing at Cedar Hall shortly before Douglass died, and he attended Booker T. Washington's funeral. His autobiography stands as a rich lens on a key period in American history. Because it is a Black perspective and because it is an account previously unavailable to scholars and the general public, it assumes even greater importance. He lived in a time of extreme racial segregation, and many of the white people with whom he worked, however friendly they might have been to him, did not talk about him in their own writings. Now that his life and works are becoming accessible (Ronnick, 2005), the many circumstances of his survival and success also are coming to light.

In order to understand how the four men in this study survived and even excelled I must look at the social structure and culture of the era when they were growing up. Specifically, the Deep South of the 1940's and 1950's invites our attention. Thereby I will build up a context for better grasping these men's lived experiences. During Jim Crow when the four African American men and I were growing up, Black teachers established respect and trusting relationships with Black students as well as with their parents in order to improve educational outcomes.

Education

The life-world and lived experiences of Black teachers grew out of slavery and the Reconstruction. Back then, Black teachers undertook to *lift as they climb*. Not surprising, though, is that many northern White teachers believed the Black teachers to be uneducated and unsophisticated (Fairclough, 2007).

Between 1925 and 1955, African Americans continued to struggle for quality education for their children. The four men's narratives of self-sacrifice and neighborhood effort offer encouragement. Their stories, from a former sharecropper to a retired school superintendent, help us appreciate how the Black community's dedication provided quality education despite racism (Gill, 2000).

Back then, it was no difficult matter for the four men as well as the Black school to construct a life-world of academic achievement. While they realistically accepted Jim Crow, overcrowded classrooms, and outdated books, they did not accept stereotypes about their inferiority. Despite the imposed substandard conditions, the socialization process meant to inculcate White values often failed to generate false identities. Black teachers and parents vigorously encouraged academic success and generally ignored institutionalized notions about the education of Black students (Evahn, Kratzer & Mc Call, 1992). Historically, then, African Americans placed great importance on education as the key to success

15

(Herbers, 1973).

This commitment to education may help to account for the historical reality that when public expenditures for African American schools in the southern states decreased significantly, most African Americans living there nevertheless became literate. African Americans themselves made heroic efforts to counteract institutional racism through an extensive system of private, self supported schools founded mostly by contributions (Books & Franklin, 1984). Ensuring the survival of these schools fell heavily on African American communities, which worked effectively to keep them open. The national African American illiteracy rate tumbled from 70% in 1880 to about 30% in 1910 (Cornelius, 1991). For African Americans, education had become a source of self-determination (Cornelius).

While many African Americans were poor and uneducated themselves, they created educational institutions for their children within two years after the first school for Whites opened in the South. The first colored school was built around 1807. It offered Sunday school classes as well as regular classes in the late afternoons during the week. African American males in particular placed great importance on education because they saw it was the key to their success (United States Office of Education, 1969).

Separate schools for African Americans were often in secluded locations, with little school equipment and few teachers. Funding for African American education was paltry, and textbooks were scarce (Brooks and Sedlacek, 1976). When they were available for African American students, the books were often outdated or even obsolete as well as damaged, with pages missing or falling out.

Yet as we have seen, rates of African American literacy continued to grow

steadily, sometimes even dramatically (Brooks & Sedlacek). Moreover, high-

achieving African American male students had relatively strong positive self-

perceptions and were able to pursue their basic needs for achievement,

acknowledgment, and autonomy (Davidson & Greenberg, 1967).

Desegregation was supposed to lead to equal educational opportunities and

freedom of choice for African Americans. Instead, many African American

neighborhood schools were abruptly put out of existence (McGroarty, 1996).

Moreover, desegregation changed the collective struggle and the united will of

African Americans (Alloway & Cordasco, 1970). Some of their anger comes from

having replaced feelings of frustration with resentment (Gordon, 2002; Miles,

1989; Upchurch, 1996).

One may wonder what impact segregated inferior schools had on African-

American men. How did inequality of education affect their hopes and dreams? It

seems that discrimination and injustice anchored their life-world. Many Black

men of my generation saw little or no chance of surviving beyond the next week

or the next year (Pasquini, 2002). I even recall having heard President Kennedy's

task force on poverty indicate that the chances of young Black men escaping

poverty were zero. To think and dream beyond the next day or the next year was

out of the ordinary, even mysterious. We were regarded and treated as outsiders

or "others" (Stewart, 1991; Lockwood, 1970). By now, some evidence suggests

that African American male students who do less well in high school are often rebelling against curricula they see as irrelevant to their life-world (Asumah & Perkins, 2001). Consequently, many African American male students dropout of school.

Family and Community

During the 1940's and the 1950's our Black community was safe enough that some parents let their children sleep outside near the front doorstep. Residents often hung their wash in shared courtyards, and sometimes relatives or friends would take down each other's clothes after work. Most of the time, though, their children would do it after school. This was the kind of life-world that I and my African-American male participants knew and remember. It even extended to cities such as Philadelphia where the Richard Allen housing project was home to a thriving Black community (Williams, 1996).

The extended Black family has been the primary institution for the survival of Black people (Hill, 2005; Bright, 1994). During slavery, many African-American families were structured into an extended family system based on birth and shared oppressive experiences (Staples, 1998; Banks, 1987; Irvin, 1992). When their parents were sold, slaves' children were reared by the older members of the extended family (Hill; Aaron, 1999; Mithun, 1973). The functions of African American kinship groups were so important that many non-relatives were referred to as family members. The extended family thus exhibited flexibility and adaptability as well as strength (Mithun).

"Fictive kin" is the common term for this pattern, which continues to this day. The African American men in *Slim's Table* thought that their life-world of community closeness or "fictive kin" was declining, but these men rediscovered such closeness among some of their friends (Duneier,1992). They learned from each other about survival and success as African American males. Like the Black family back then, their group of friends was fundamentally a supportive extended family who identified with hegemonic values without being fully accepted in mainstream society (Scott, 1997).

The Black extended family's strengths also included a strong achievement orientation and a strong work orientation, plus strong spiritual support (Hill,1998), which further heightened the prospects for survival. In fact, one role of the extended Black family was to ensure that young African American males accomplish something in life (Herndon & Hirt, 2004).

Historically and still today, the extended Black family has played a significant role not only in promoting educational achievement but also in reducing behavior problems among African American males (Rodney & Tachia, 1998; Coleman & Shaw, 2002; Staples, 1998). The African American life-world can to some extent be seen as a self-governing world largely disconnected from White mainstream society. Within their world Black families often become self-sustaining microcommunties.

Each such family is equivalent to a community within a community involving what has been called "living behind the veil." It was a way to sustain African American culture (Rodney & Tachia,1998; Coleman & Shaw, 2002;

Staples, 1998). Together, the Black extended family and the community generally favored an uplifting pedagogy that eased burdens and fed hope (Hill, 2005; Aaron, 1999; Bright, 1994). Even though racial uplift centered on the extended Black family, religious organizations promoted means of survival in a racist society (Frate, Shimkin, D. & E. Shimkin, 1978), it has sometimes been seen as disorganized, unstable, or even pathological (Toliver, 1982). The ethnography *Slim's Table* (Duneier,1992) mentioned above serves as a counterpoint to such portrayals.

Slim's Table (Duneier,1992) is a study of working-class African American men who gather at the Valois Cafeteria on Chicago's South Side. It is a scholarly look at African American life in the inner city. Duneier, the sociologist who did this study, argues that these men constitute a caring community together whose moral values contradict widespread stereotypes about African American men's life-world. Their community takes shape around the table at the eatery that for more than a decade has been their daily meeting place (Morgan, 1993). These Black men grew up in homes where fathers were present. They are consistently inner-directed and committed, and they act with self-determination; their self-esteem rests neither on material assets nor the endorsement of mainstream society.

Yet, Duneier emphasizes that even social scientists misrepresent the life-world of such African American men and thus help to perpetuate stereotypes about them. Researchers must struggle against their own stereotypical beliefs and become involved in African American men's life-world so as to understand what sorts of community and family supports they have fashioned for themselves

(Duneier, 1992). Researchers must also see whether their concepts fit the life-world of these individuals. They should also closely read African-American males' narratives in order to understand how they make sense of their world (Toliver, 1982). To know people's world means to know their stories, including all the trials and turning points that have tested them and how their many experiences have shaped them (Ibarra & Lineback, 2005).

The Black Church

The history of African-American Christianity is bound up with the history of slavery. It was as slaves that they began the long process of making Christianity their own (Campbell, 1998). Historically, the Black church has promoted survival and freedom. It created an array of beliefs particularly designed to meet the distinctive needs of African-American families (Gregory, Long & Volk, 2004; Harvey, 2005); It thus developed a theology of hope and uplift (Harvey, 2005). African American churches historically have reached out to Black families in times of need.

Restricted and denied educational opportunities, African American preachers elaborated on Bible narratives in imaginative ways that were meaningful to their congregations (Mitchell, 1990). By and large, they carefully avoided provoking their congregations to resist slavery and suffer defeat. Thus, spirituals or cries became the expression of resistance that pervaded African Americans' life-world. Spirituals were the expressions of a subjugated people that symbolized hope as well as joys and sorrows (Guillory, 1974).

Phenomenologically, then, the African American church created a life-world of hope in the midst of slavery and oppression (Smith, 1985).
The Black church uplifted a people deprived of their humanity (Nelson, 2005). Historically, through diverse paths, it has been culturally receptive to the daily necessities of African American males as well as females. The African American preachers reminded listeners, for example, how they have succeed in spite of injustices and horrors (Andrews, 2002; Thompson, 1954). Early on, the Black church became a supporter of education and later, more overtly, a protester of civil rights violations and injustices. The Negro church also served as a community welfare agency and provided Christian education (Blackwell, 1991; Youngblood & Winn, 2004).

By 1900, the Black church supported over 80 elementary and high schools (Quarles, 1964). Throughout the 1940's and the 1950's, the African American church continued to play a vital role in the lives of its members. It served as central location for community participation, instruction, and religious worship. Their church provided African Americans a spiritual community counteracting institutionalized racism (Youngblood & Winn, 2004). Involvement in church life was and remains very important for African-American males today.

More than three-fourths of African Americans believe that churches should engage in social change (Youngblood & Winn, 2004). In fact, many places of worship spawned informal networks that strengthen and encourage people engaged in civil disobedience (Nelson, 2005). Moreover, church-based networks increased the likelihood of Blacks becoming political activists. For example, being active on church boards and being involved in church-based political communication correlates with increasing Black involvement in both electoral and nonelectoral politics (Ginwright, 2002; cf. Blackwell, 1991; Nelson ; Vivian, 1970; Jennings, 2003). In traditional African American culture, then, life is not sharply separated into spheres of influence designated as sacred and secular (Costen, 2001).

Yet many times the Black church did falter on its promise to address the needs of African American men during the 1940's and the 1950's. Back then, there were great opportunities along those lines for African American churches. A generation ago, for instance, four out of five inner-city African American men had some contact with church or Sunday school (Pinn, 2002; Jennings, 2003; Vivian, 1970). Today, however, Blacks may be less knowledgeable about looking beyond their present circumstances and envisioning self-determination. They may be unaware of their church as a life-line of hope unaware, then, of its long-established religious praxis, its prayers and its Negro spirituals (Overacker, 1998; Vivian).

Back then, as we have seen, Negro spirituals were distinctive songs of hope, a supporting mechanism that produced a liberating calmness within the souls of Black folks. Negro spirituals were more than spiritual narratives and vivid images of a people subject to terror, racism, and oppression; these spirituals reinforced their faith and provided a sense of empowerment (Stewart, 1997). Frazier implied that living under oppressive conditions, Black people sang the

23

blues and moaned the spirituals. "Sometime I Feel like a Moaning Dove" and "Nobody Knows the Trouble I Sees" was the essence of their life-world back then. Negroes poured their mourning into songs and expressed their emotions with an all-consuming feeling. Although the Negro spirituals were moaned, hummed, and shouted out among others who were empathetic, the blues helped African Americans overcome their sense of powerlessness and their inability to protect loved ones.

The messages of the past should help Black youths overcome their sense of alienation and despair. Throughout the Jim Crow era Black people did not give up their mourning work; Negro spirituals were still recognized as means of psychological and spiritual healing. Instead of giving up their spirituals and mourning work, they institutionalized them in their churches, extended families, and even their poetry (Martin, E. & J. Martin, 1995). Similar to the four African American men, Black people back then articulated a volatile life-world of absurdities, contradictions, and humor. I was inspired to capture their sense of discrepancies and humor, therefore I am the author of these poems.

Black Jesus,

White Jesus

Brown or blue

You have to love me!

Before he loves you.

Maybe,

He left before slavery,

Or

Long_____ before Katrina

Maybe,

He left before the riots

Or

Even Jim Crow

Maybe,

He took the interstate

Escaping the ghettoes

And fled! _____

 High rent and rats, and toxic waste

And maybe

 Police brutality

Come by here lord!

Come by here.

He ain't here just now,

He left long ago____

He ain't picking cotton,

Not now,

Not any more.

Disappeared,

 Vanished!

Gone!

to the Suburbs.

African American Males and Leadership

The life-world of the four men during the 1940's and the 1950's included sit-ins, kneel-ins, picket lines, economic boycotts, and elective buying campaigns. A new style of Black leadership was emerging. This new Negro leadership emerged in the middle of World War II and further developed during the second half of the twentieth century. These new Black leaders were neither compliant and indebted to White people nor uneducated and restricted to traditional forms of protest against the status quo. Their goal was nothing less than full and equal opportunity as Americans.

When the four men and I were growing up, though, the old Negro middle-class leadership still held sway. Unlike the later Black leadership, the old Negro middle-class leadership had much to lose by desegregation. Its life-world revolved around a small society of Black business and professionals. They lived within a secretive closed society but always within the borders of the Black community (Pfautz, 1963).

Within our segregated life-world back then, African American educators were often accepted as leaders in the community. Many of them were self-made men attuned to the educational needs of African American males (McGee and Neufeldt, 1990). Although it is common to regard Frederick Douglas' antebellum struggle for literacy as exceptional, interviews with former slaves as well as other accounts suggest more extensive communities of learners who understood the link between literacy and self-determination (Williams, 1996).

Historically, African American leadership thus belonged to trustworthy *race men* and women who led community institutions, including not only Black schools and the Black church but also businesses and social and civic organizations. This model of African American leadership was predominately masculine. It was also successful, accommodating, authoritarian and autocratic back then (Sullivan, 1997).

African American men's civic engagement remains crucial. The traditional hierarchical model of Black leadership must give way to more collaborative leadership, though. Above all, this new kind of leadership must make full use of the rich social capital of inner-city African American males (Sullivan, 1997; Blackwell, 1991; Ginwright, 2002; Nelson, 2005). Put differently, what we need is people interested less in being leaders and more in developing leadership in others. One study that suggests a school-centered approach focused at nine African American underprivileged schools in North Carolina where African American achievement was especially high. Teacher-leaders in these schools developed a culture of achievement and used various mechanisms for communicating high expectations not only to students but also to parents (North Carolina State Department of Public Instruction, 2000).

Back then when the four men and I were growing up, such a culture of achievement was internalized at home and reinforced by our own teacher-leaders.

As we will see, the four men lament the loss of closeness, acceptance and recognition rooted in such a culture (Shingles, 1979). Although Jim Crow, racial barriers, and inequality of opportunities restricted our social and economic participations in mainstream society, our shared resources and our strong leaders encouraged us to make progress.

It was essential back then for Black leaders and kinfolk to provide emotional and economic support for our survival and success (Barnes, 2003). Authentic Black leaders back then led by inspiration and example. Fear of competition was out of place. Black parents and Black leaders held hands across generational, educational and social barriers. Today, Black leaders articulate equal opportunity and equal access, but we should always ask above all, what they are doing for Black people (Dickerson, 2004). The four men's narratives, lived experiences and dialogues offer insights into Black leadership back then as well as right now.

The four men and I have noticed the absence of Black leadership within the Black community today. Back then, Black leaders consistently embraced the symbols of Black manhood and strong figures who demonstrated superior ability (Stanfield, 1993). Disheartened by existing Black leadership, the four men agreed that with the help of strong, innovative leaders we should continue overcoming the false, imposed identity of inferiority. Back then, we constructed a life-world that prevented much psychologically destructive behavior. A pedagogy of racial uplift prevailed back then but has largely vanished. Black leaders today aim for political power rather than social and economic justice (Barnes, 2003).

Black leaders today need to focus on what is achievable rather than what is unachievable. This focus should begin within the Black family and then outward to the Black community. No group, however dominant, can resist the force of a people committed to family but, most of all, committed to excellence (Dickerson, 2004). The four men understand how Black leaders and the Black family interacted to advance our collective concerns (Rosenberg, 1966). They also understand that today's Black leaders must carry on the tradition of recognizing that racism is not responsible for Black men ambushing their neighbor, dropping out of school, underachieving, giving in to despair or settling for a life less than what it can be with hard work and racial pride (Dickerson).

A Personal Epilogue

There was nothing unusual about our lives growing up as African American males. We were facing ups and downs, pleasures and threats like everyone else in our community. Throughout our hardships we tried to hold fast to the belief that everything happens for a reason. At times life was simple and at other times difficult, but it was always challenging. Upon reflection it always seems that no matter how bad the circumstances seemed to be at the time, the end result was our greatest interest. Our hopes were severely tested, and questions haunted us as we tried to make sense of our oppression. We knew that we could not allow our disappointments and failures to dampen our spirits or to shake our faith. We had to believe that God had a purpose for us so we continued on our path.

Our efforts to overcome doubts and fears and move beyond the racial barriers in our path moved us forward. This was perhaps the most extraordinary part of our lived experiences. Though many of us were strangers brought together by horrible circumstances and lived experiences, sharing our feelings made us realize that we were not alone. We did not know how much longer we would be able to hold to our beliefs, yet we were afraid to give up hope. If we gave up hope, it would be tantamount to accepting the certainty of living as inferior beings. We had done all that we were supposed to do and had applied all that we knew to do. Yet many of us still had to learn how to overcome our own false consciousness. We had to see life from a Biblical perspective, knowing that all things are possible.

CHAPTER III

METHODS

In this chapter I present the major elements of the phenomenological methodology used in my study. Qualitative research embraces the phenomenological approach that includes philosophical assumptions as well as methods of generating and analyzing data. Phenomenology focuses on knowledge and understanding of individuals' lived experiences; it insists on respect for how individuals perceive and experience their life-worlds (Schwandt, 2001). My objective is fundamentally phenomenological, namely, to explore in detail four African-American men's life-world.

Phenomenologists assume that the life-world is the primary focus of study in the human sciences. The everyday world or the *life-world* is the intersubjective world of human experience and social action; it is the world of commonsense awareness of everyday life (Manen, 2002). This life-world encompasses the thoughts and acts of individuals as well as their shared expressions about those thoughts and actions. A phenomenological approach discloses what a life-world consists of, including the beliefs that give it structure (Schwandt, 2001). This philosophical standpoint is capable of repudiating modernist metanarratives about the lived experiences of African American males. Therefore, it is imperative for one to realize there is knowledge outside of one's live world.

A postmodernist perspective with its emphasis on texts and discourses can serve as an effective complement to phenomenology. In particular, the postmodernist emphasis on the narratives makes this perspective helpful here. Narrative is a means of telling a story that links the past, present, and future. A narrative makes cultures, societies, and historical eras understandable as wholes; it reveals parts of these complex, inconsistent wholes. A narrative can even stimulate civic participation about social issues by disclosing how personal problems illustrate public issues and by illuminating both collective identity and collective solutions (Seidman, 1998; Biber & Leavy, 2004; Lormand, 1996).

My approach involves attention to the details in the participants' own accounts about their world. My approach also involves paying close attention to the participants' reserved and guarded expressions that may disclose personal sufferings, perhaps kept hidden for decades. These men's controlled expressions may be a shield, for example, or an emotional fortification (Manen, 2002). Questions arise throughout the study about how these men perceived themselves in the past amidst overt segregation and oppression. I remain alert to what stimulated or encouraged them to sustain an effective but perhaps agonizing journey toward self-determination.

Although my study focuses on the life-world of four African American males, it in no way discounts the efforts and achievements of African American women in uplifting the African American community. As an African American male who grew up in the 1940's and the 1950's, I am, though, more concerned with the dilemmas of African American males, especially how they were able to survive productively against great odds. My focus lies specifically with their experiences of family, religion, community, educational leadership, and mentoring.

My inquiry uses the inductive approach to participants' statements and claims which is typical in a comparative case study. Such inductive work also occurred during my analysis of historical data. Yet my data were not out there somewhere ready to be gathered like fruit from a tree. Data are generated or created within theoretical frameworks and research designs. What becomes data depends on the researcher's intentions and questions (Lormand, 1996).

The participants' stories allowed me to learn about their life-world and focus on their realities. All this learning involved self-reflection as well as viewing the world from the participants' perspectives (Schwandt, 2001). Their respective narratives explained how they found meaning and purpose in life and how they came to accept responsibility for what their lives had been and are still becoming. The opposite of such a life-world involves estrangement, objectification, and alienation, which by definition strip a person not only of a sense of responsibility but also of purpose in life (Schwandt, 2001).

It was important for me to understand how the four men's stories were told, organized, developed, and even where they began. It was also important that I attune myself to what was being implied as well as what was obvious in their narratives. I was able to find themes, to see patterns and shared meanings among the participants. Individuals in oppressive circumstances often share core beliefs, yet at the same time they clearly disagree about certain aspects of their life-world (Lormand, 1996; Schwandt, 2001). Looking for both convergent and divergent meanings among the four participants was crucial to inferring their mundane pedagogy and everyday praxis (Lormand).

Access and Trust

For qualitative researchers, access is a dynamic process that requires establishing rapport with participants in order to learn from them (Bell, Berger & Feldman, 2003). Further, researchers are often asking participants to speak about politically and personally sensitive matters so a close working relationship is essential. So is trust. Otherwise some individuals will withhold their insights (Berson, 1994). I made copies of the University of West Florida's Intuitional Review Board approval forms and explained to the participants that I am constrained by the university and its guidelines as well as by our years of friendship. I provided these documents and explained my purpose at the beginning of the interview process. The participants shared some apprehension about my project. To reduce their fears of being identified, I made clear I would fully protect their anonymity. They became more assured as we moved forward in the interview process.

As I began generating data, my identity quickly changed from a doctoral researcher to a regular African American male neighbor. I found my dual position very difficult. I wanted to respond as a fellow African American male rather than as a researcher. I had to think critically about my experiences, especially since the strain of going back and forth between the two roles was great at times. Our interviews, conversations, and exchange of ideas caused some of the most difficult moments during the research. I listened attentively to the four men, though.

Before the interviewing and tape recording began, I was an insider, a homeboy, a homey, a fellow collaborator, an equal, a member of the team. As soon as I clicked Record, I became a researcher, an outsider, and perhaps even a representative of the White man or the *Man*. For a while, I became an insider/outsider or what Patricia Hill Collins (2000) calls an *insider within*. These four men finally accepted me as a member of the Black community, but at the same time I felt largely excluded from their innermost world of emotions, hardships, and disappointments. This exclusion was somewhat of a disappointment since I had known several of these men since childhood.

After ending each recording, instantly I became once again an insider, a member of the group as in the early days. Slowly, the men's language and their tone of voice changed. They became more open and affectionate. Over the period of the interviewing process, I asked myself whether I was an effective interviewer or researcher. Was I making any identical mistakes? At times, especially during the early interviews, I felt like a police officer or an investigator instead of a friend and researcher.

Interviews

I interviewed the four participants and also drew on historical data from the scholarly literature to understand how similar persons overcame oppression and segregation (Lormand, 1996). Those of us who aim to understand and document participants' life-world often favor semi-structured interviewing. Such interviewing provides a framework for exploring the experiences of research participants while granting their perspectives privileged status of authenticity. All we have as qualitative researchers are narratives, some from other people, some from ourselves, some from archives and other sources. Qualitative researchers try to appreciate how and where these narratives are created, what types of stories they entail, and how we can put them to truthful and scholarly uses to understand and theorize about social life (Seidman,1998).

Since my objective was to learn in detail about these men's life-world, I did four in-depth semistructured interviews with each participant for 50-75 minutes each (Schwandt, 2001). In each interview I addressed particular issues and touched upon diverse aspects of the men's life-world. The best way to ask questions is to let people answer in their own terms, voicing their own views, values, and experiences. Often, my questions were phrased to elicit accounts about their fears, conflicts, and accomplishments. Sometimes particular words or phases that the participants used were important keys to understanding their life-world and lived experiences. The following questions are a few examples of how I queried the participants:

1. What were your major duties as a father?

2. What do you think about Black leadership today?

3. How might your nurturing during childhood have influenced your

   attitudes and values?

4. How has the Black family changed since your childhood?

5. What motivated you to succeed in life?

6. Why do you think some African-American males are not succeeding today?

7. How important was religion in your family?

8. How did you or your family deal with inequality of opportunity for

   African Americans?

9. What are your attitudes about education?

10. Could you describe your teachers before integration?

    Your community?

11. Could you describe some of the biggest challenges facing

    African American males?

I reproduce poetic transcriptions for my dissertation, and my first one is in chapter IV. Poetic transcriptions are intended to stimulate readers' reactions and constructive representations (American Evaluation Association, 2000). In poetic transcription the researcher makes use of interview data to make freestyle poetry from the lived experiences of others as reported in their own words (Carr, 2003). Alternatively, it is the construction of poemlike compositions from the verbal communications, expressions and vernacular of interviewees (Glesne, 1997).

Poetic transcription is a new postmodernist type of writing that materialized in the 1980's. It allowed African American writers to illustrate and tell about their perplexities in fresh ways. Poetic transcription gives birth to new kinds of narrative meaningfulness. Poetic transcription can, for example, incorporate apparent constitute digressions into a framework that describe vestiges of the past that coexist with the present. Because students come from many different cultures, postmodernists teachers can use poetic transcriptions to let students write in ways that convey their feelings and emotions about their life-world and lived experiences (Sweeney, 2007). Thus, poetic transcription is useful beyond the realm of research.

Triangulation and Member Checks

Triangulation is a process whereby researchers enhance the authenticity of their studies (Guion, 2002). It also serves as a check on the credibility of the conclusions or findings a researcher offers. Triangulation entails the use of various theoretical perspectives, several methods, or multiple data sources, or all of these.

Since every research method has limitations, good research usually involves multiple methods. Triangulation can strengthen a study not only by using several methods but also by incorporating more than one theoretical perspective to interpret the data and thereby enhance legitimacy (Patton, 2002). Triangulation adds breadth and depth to an analysis. Qualitative researchers seeks an enriched approach to their topic through triangulation (Denzin & Lincoln, 2003).

As part of my triangulation, in addition to interviewing, I explored archival records. For example, I searched for historical information in African American newspapers, books, and journals, for instance, *The Journal of Black Studies*, and *The Journal of Negro History*. My theoretical triangulation involves not only phenomenology and postmodernism but also Afrocentric perspectives. Another measure of enhancing the quality of my data and my data analysis was member checks.

Member checks are also called member or respondent corroboration. Typically, these involve soliciting feedback from participants on the researcher's data or findings (Schwandt, 2001). I undertook member checks by summarizing my findings and giving the summary to all participants to confirm that my interpretation of the data reflected what they had endeavored to convey (Denzin & Lincoln, 2003).

This postmodernist perspective is a process of discovery and inquiry. It is important for the researcher to appropriately decide what to exclude and how to present the remaining material given the masses of data (Biber & Leavy, 2004). The qualitative researcher faces the daunting task of making sense of what has been discovered, but the art of illumination entails making sense of what the researcher has learned (Biber & Leavy). For this reason, member checking and insightfully, creatively interpreting interview data are vital in capturing authentic expressions unfamiliar to outsiders, thus revealing hidden or unfamiliar realities (Schwandt, 2001). This process enhances understanding of the participants' lived experiences and life-world.

I should not attempt to analyze these men's life-world from the standpoint of an outsider. My standpoint is that of an insider or an emic standpoint. *Emic* refers to personal experiences in the life-world as opposed to standing outside it (etic). It includes experiences of idioms, ideas, and even body language used within a particular group. An emic framework provides for getting as close as possible to the immediacy of lived experiences (Schwandt, 2001).

Given the plan to incorporate considerable triangulation and substantial member checks, I did not specify the full design at the outset of the study. Instead, emergent design characterizes qualitative inquiry. Such a fluid design involves keeping pace with and adapting to what participants actually do, know, believe, and experience. It also involves fine tuning the theoretical propositions and understandings whatever materializes. The qualitative researcher requires substantial flexibility and adaptability and should avoid getting locked into rigid designs. Qualitative researchers need to accommodate unanticipated findings as they emerge (Patton, 2002).

Participants

I selected these four African American males for several reasons. They experienced a legally segregated school system, and also went to school in the same dilapidated buildings that I attended. Also, I wanted to closely examine the larger life-world of African American men during the 1940's and the 1950's. Many who have written about African American males have never themselves experienced an oppressive life-world. As an insider, I seek to elicit insights into the spirit of four African American men. Their narratives may be reflective of others who established a faith in God or some other gospel of deliverance. These four African American men may reveal a profound pedagogy illustrating that God did not declare them failures or victims (Thompson, 1954).

My inquiry focuses not only on these four African American men's narratives and pedagogy but also on their praxis, which involves community responsibility and a shared ideology (Schwandt, 2001). Their life-world was a paradox of challenges between what was expected of them as individuals and what was expected of them as African-Americans (Biber & Leavy, 2004). Perhaps they attempted to live in two worlds (Schwandt; Biber and Leavy; Mariampolski, 2001).

Again, the participants' real names are safeguarded (Rubenstein and Bloch, 1982). I introduce these men with the following pseudonyms: Mr. Curtis, Mr. Leon, Mr. Dwight, and Mr. Lee.

Reflections on My Own Lived Experiences

As I reflect upon these men's lived experiences, I relive my own family stories. My own voice resonates the four African American men's voices that have significantly been silenced in mainstream society. In spite of our ability to survive and construct meaning for our lives, our right to be heard has largely gone unrecognized (Haskins, 1992). As we have seen, postmodernist writing captures lost or silenced voices (Pazaratz, 2004; Biber & Leavy, 2004). Thereby empowerment becomes possible.

In my generation, though, African American men learned to empower themselves and to enhance their self-esteem by fighting racism while becoming

41

successful. Our life-world was a reality few Whites know. For example, in the 1940's and the 1950's, Black instructors had graduated from predominantly white universities and had been educated during the Great Depression. Regularly and persistently, they presented excessive amounts of textbook material and research work. They also wanted African Americans, especially male students, to survive and even do well within mainstream society. They had no reservations about encouraging Black students to realize their potential and to assist others reach their goals.

These Black instructors seldom displayed sympathy or understanding, but at the same time they were not indifferent or insensitive to their students' psychological needs. They believed that it was their duty to prepare their students for life's struggles. In many respects, the 1940's and 1950's were supposed to have been an astonishing time of achievement and social mobility for African-Americans. There was the post-World War II boom with a demand for skilled and unskilled employment as well as for academic positions. Amazingly, many African American males began to take advantage of the limited opportunities available to them, and their upward mobility was becoming a large-scale reality. The increased enrollment in Black colleges for African American males was not surprising to us who had the same dream of becoming successful (Wilson, 1990). As in other Black communities, the means of upward mobility was usually higher education (Glasgow, 1980).

Despite much educational advancement, African American males are still facing the inequality of education (Lomotey, 1990; Roscigno, 1998). The dual and inferior education today is nothing like what the four men and I experienced. In many ways our school was a home away from home, not a place of alienation and indifference. Inequality of education and denial of opportunities are a continuing lived experience for most African American students (Kain, 2004; College, Georgia & Gibson, 1992; Lipton & Oakes, 1999; Renninger & Steiner, 1993). Throughout much of American history we have had two societies, two communities and two school systems (Kain). Consequently, we have had two life-worlds, one of White privilege and the other of marginalization.

Ethics and Limitations of the Study

Ethics are an integral part of social research. Informed consent, voluntary participation, and confidentiality were among the main considerations that I as a qualitative researcher encountered. I was required to have signed written consent forms from the participants whom I interviewed (Siegle, 2004).The consent forms (see appendix B) ensured that the interviewees' participation was voluntary, that they were free to decline to answer any question at any time and that they were free to withdraw from the interview or even from the study at any time. The consent form affirmed that their interviews would be kept confidential, that the interview transcript would not be accessible to anyone besides me, and that their identities would not be revealed.

Quotes from the interviews are part of the final research study, but under no circumstances are names or any identifying information included with them (Siegle). These and other ethical matters should be well

43

thought out, especially when giving voice to those who have been marginalized (Schwandt, 2001).

To articulate in a public discourse involves ethical and political obligations. As a researcher, I must be familiar with the ethical issues and moral dilemmas of my inquiry and also held accountable for any fallout (Denzin & Lincoln, 2003). Qualitative study requires continuous consideration about confidentiality and the protection of participants' identities. Confidentiality is considered a given in ethical research, and the participants must make an informed decision to participate in the research, which means that they understand the researcher's aims (Biber & Leavy, 2004). In my case, however, ethically sensitive issues were inevitable because of my special closeness with the four participants.

As an insider, I expected to cultivate compassion and trust with the participants. This undertaking seemed not to present much of a challenge since we shared experience of overt oppression, inferior schools and closeness within the Black community (Biber & Leavy, 2004). The participants identified with and related to an era of survival, daily struggles, hunger, sacrifice and sharing. As a member of this group, then, I thought I knew enough about the phenomenon under study to ask appropriate questions. Yet, as a researcher, I did not take for granted that the four men fully understood all of my questions (Silverman, 1997; Pazaratz, 2004).

My task is to enlighten readers about the life-world of these men with depth and detail from their perspectives and to portray their meanings (Silverman,

1997; Denzin & Lincon, 2003). Insights into their social worlds were derived mostly from interviewing. As a researcher, I faced the question of what to make of my data. I did not know which details within their narratives would turn out to be important and helpful for the analysis (Silverman).

These four African American men revealed attitudes that clashed with what people commonly take for granted about what African American men ought to be, do and say (Silverman, 1997; Biber & Leavy, 2004). Collectively, their narratives challenge popular stereotypes about African American men (Silverman; Biber & Leavy; Denzin & Lincoln, 2003). Their narratives cannot be generalized to other narratives in comparable surroundings, but they nevertheless give voice to those who have been silenced or marginalized.

Some narratives may be scrambled, disorganized or perplexing, and there may be limitations in trying to make sense of them (Frank, 1995). This can occur when researchers try to understand the life-world of others. As one might expect, within most storytellers' narratives, which of necessity must be fragmented to some extent. I describe accurate but delimited segments about the lived experiences of the participants, but in doing so, I have singled out and decided what was meaningful and central. Many groups do not want themselves exposed more or less in their totality (Silverman, 1997; Schram, 2003; Mariampolski, 2001). As an insider, I was mindful and sensitive to these and other concerns (Silverman).

CHAPTER IV

FINDINGS

Family and Community

When I was growing up, most Black families lived in two worlds, the life-world of White people and the life-world of Black people. The Black families I typically knew refused to accept economic limitations and negative images about themselves. In spite of being oppressed and marginalized, Black parents routinely instilled a sense of self-worth and dignity in their children and did not allow them to settle for second best or to be educationally deficient.

By exploring the life-worlds of four African American men from such families, I expect to enlighten readers. Their narratives express both self-respect and racial pride as well as other themes. First, I introduce the four men whose experiences are the focus of this study. I introduce each individual in detail. Since these men are relatively prominent in their community, I am extremely vigilant about not revealing anything more than is necessary. As I have already implied, these four men all grew up in a Black segregated community in northwest Florida before the era of integration, Food Stamps and the Free School Lunch program. Family closeness and community unity were the norm back then, according to their responses, and church going was a way of life.

Their Black teachers knew them and usually their parents, too, as friends, neighbors, or church members. As young students, they had to walk three to four miles to school, even when White students had access to school buses. It was counted as a blessing if I or one of the four men was fortunate enough to buy a car while in high school. Now I present these men's profiles so that you can glimpse their life-world and perhaps understand how they were determined to overcome inferior schools and outdated schoolbooks. I want to give you some sense of each individual while maintaining their anonymity, which is ethically obligatory for me.

The Four Men

Mr. Leon is a retired school teacher, administrator, and grandfather in his late 60's. He often keeps his grandson and involves himself in all his grandson's activities. Mr. Leon's greatest joy besides playing golf is devoting a great deal of time to his grandson, a teenager who plays on baseball and football teams. Mr. Leon takes him to every game, even the out of town ones. For whatever reasons, he does not want his grandson traveling alone with his teammates. I suppose he is protective of his grandson. Mr. Leon lights up when he boasts to his neighbors about the events and outings he and his grandson enjoy together. His wife of more than 30 years does not journey with them.

Mr. Leon does volunteer work for the Baptist church where he is a very faithful member. I did not know him very well growing up because he was a little older than I, but I was aware that he and his family were committed church members. Church going was also the way he raised his children. He and his wife have one son and one daughter, both college graduates. Mr. Leon went to college part-time during the same period when his children were at college on scholarships. Over the years, Mr. Leon slowly earned his master's degree. He never considered his degree remarkable. He believed and was taught by his parents that if you want something in life, all you have to do is apply yourself, nothing more and nothing less.

Neither his mother nor his father finished high school, but they taught him to have a purpose in life. They also taught him that religion and education were the means to a better life for self and family. Needless to say, he went to a segregated Black school, but its inferior quality never troubled Mr. Leon because he believed that the teachers did their best with what they had. He believes that if Black students really wanted to learn, all they had to do was apply themselves to achieve their goals. Mr. Leon's home has been paid off for years, and his children are doing very well. They are all living peacefully and very happily.

Mr. Dwight is in his mid 60's and differs from the other three men in coming from a small middle-class family. He had only one brother and one sister, and his parents did not let him associate closely with many males in the African American community. As a teenager, for instance, he was not allowed to stay out late at night like many of his peers. Mr. Dwight was very close to his family, but such closeness at that time was not unusual. While we were growing up, frequently a few young Black men would call him mama's boy because he would not do things a number of them did. He always seemed to have a job working for his father who had several different kinds of jobs. I got to know his father because he used to cut my hair on weekends.

I worked with Mr. Dwight until he went off to college. Even though he was a year or so older than I, I used to protect him from a few young Black men in the neighborhood who were continually teasing him and looking for a fight. All the while, I respected Mr. Dwight a lot because he was one of few young men I personally knew who was doing something constructive with his life. Before long, however, I found many more African American males who had the same educational dreams and hopes of a better future as we had.

Everyone in the community knew Mr. Dwight was going to become successful. He is now a retired school teacher and administrator. He is divorced. Mr. Dwight married an outsider, a young lady not from the South. One cold night she just left. "Well, it is a good thing they had no children," everyone remarked. I suspect he has never really gotten over his divorce because of how much he values marriage, home, family, his Baptist church, and togetherness. Mr. Dwight became a mentor and a leader in his church as well as in various Black organizations. Although he is living by himself and has never remarried, he is pleased with his life. He is very well respected and liked.

Mr. Curtis is in his late 50's and is currently working in the school system. He looks forward to retirement so that he can spend a great deal of time trying to improve the lives of young people. He has already developed a program that has proven useful in providing guidance and direction for youth. Mr. Curtis is concerned with students from all racial/ethnic groups. He believes too many students suffer physical or psychological problems, with many virtually abandoned and left to fend for themselves.

Mr. Curtis does not believe that we can solve racial dilemmas or social problems until teachers edify students with values that supersede their lived experiences of neglect, disorder, and bewilderment. Many of our social problems, he believes, derive not from the students but from the parents who have sometimes emotionally forsaken their children. The slogan *No child left behind* has long been part of his effort to rescue as many children as possible from bureaucracy, the streets, drugs, and prison. Over the years, Mr. Curtis has seen enormous changes in his former students' lives. Many of his students are now contributing to society as parents and as community leaders.

Mr. Curtis' own experiences growing up involved love, encouragement, and support. His father and mother were always there to ensure that he and his brothers and sisters went to church and did their homework. Yet, Mr. Curtis never escaped the life-world of poverty. His family had known difficult times, but they overrode them with a sense of belonging, spirituality, and sharing. His parents always knew where their children were going, whom they were with, and what time they would be home. It was hell to pay for all involved if their parents discovered otherwise.

Mr. Curtis has three daughters, all of whom have doctoral degrees. He is very close to them. Every day, he talks to at least one of them and reflects about how he raised his daughters. When I inquired about his wife, I was kindly maneuvered toward another subject several times. Mr. Curtis often indicated, though, that he is blissfully married. He says his wife has been his biggest supporter, especially while he was earning his master's degree.

Mr. Lee is in his mid 60's and is a retired school teacher. Like most African-Americans of his generation, Mr. Lee enrolled at a predominately Black college. He has two sons and a daughter and has been married for more than 25 years. His children are college graduates and are doing very well. He and his wife are members of the same Baptist church where he grew up. Little was said about his wife, even though she had also taught school for many years. Mr. Lee is proudly involved teaching Sunday school, but other than that he seems to stay to himself. After he graduated from college, Mr. Lee did not return to his hometown for several years. He lived for a while in the northern city where his wife was born. Going away and staying for such a long period was not unusual for African American men who enlisted in the military back then, but that practice was unusual among other young Black men.

As he reflects upon where he came from, how he arrived at his current status, and the difficult times he went through growing up, Mr. Lee expresses both pleasure and sadness. He believes that some Black teachers thought he was intellectually slow, and he frequently felt marginalized. He is delighted to have accomplished what he set out to prove to himself. He has demonstrated that he is just as smart and resolute as the next person. His anguish is most reflected in his voice when he laments the unused opportunities of so many African-American young men.

Mr. Lee also laments fatherless Black families and today's loss of the

African American community as "a place of togetherness." Even when we did not have anything, we had a sense of hope and a sense of the future. That is all now gone, he believes. In spite of growing up with an unmarried mother and without any brothers or sisters, the Black community provided him emotional support. His current family consists of his divorced mother and himself.

Growing up, Mr. Lee lived across the tracks from the main Black neighborhood. His section within the Black community was somewhat an enclave, with many of the Black families living there apparently on the margins of the broader Black community. His neighborhood was thus somewhat isolated. Most of its families had a different religious affiliation than most Black families in Pensacola. Yet we all shared the same lived experiences of subjugation and segregation. As young Black men growing up, we played basketball together during the summer.

In this chapter I speak both as a member of that community during that era and as a social researcher. I do my utmost here to make clear in each instance which voice is at work as I report my findings on family and community. This chapter thus focuses foremostly on two aspects of the four participants' lives. Here I continue using the phenomenological approach that guided my research with these men.

We were one back then

Fictive family members

 Borrowing sugar

Rice and flour,

And

Even clothes--------- On special occasions

appreciation

Gently and clearly

Was always unspoken,

Back Then!

Generosity and caring

Was our life-world_____Back then.

While

Survivorship, deepen.

and

Nurtured Relationships

Shaped our identity

and

Our humanity.

Back then,

But nowadays,

Longed____ and____Buried!

Dismissed, ____ and____Dismantled.

We are……….. Simply,

Alienated………Beings

Hiding authenticity

 In private enclaves

But dare not lose

Our artificial face

Landry, 1987; Herbers). Black Families Now and Then

Passionately, the four men describe their life-world back then as a basis to

their success. Intentionally and persistently, they refer to and describe their life-

world back then as a world of relationships that entailed a clear understanding of

their identity. Yet the reasons for their success cannot be readily quantified, or

measured, or even understood. Nevertheless careful examination of the four

men's life-world back then may provide considerable insights into their

determination to move beyond their economic and social oppression. I begin with

their observations and reports about their families of origin as well as about the

families they themselves created in the context of contemporary African

American family structures. Their families of origin are, I infer, a source of or a

foundation for their success while their families of destination tend to be signs or

emblems of their success.

Thoughtfully exploring the bases of the four men's success based on

certain aspects of their lived experiences is perhaps unproductive and ineffectual

without insights into their life-world. The men's affirmations and assertions on

certain topics are thus my primary source of insights into the trajectory of their

achievements. Yet, the four men's lively specificity about certain events in their life-world does not equate to cause and effect in connection with their success. As a researcher and as an insider, though, I took serious note of what these men internalized as noteworthy in helping them succeed and what they regard as inconsequential. The possible reasons for the men's success rest not on some theoretical model or set of abstract concepts, but on my sense of the totality of a life-world of sharing, suffering, and optimism back then.

In order to appreciate the Black family, it is essential to take into account the overt racism back then and how White scholarly literature depicted the Black family during that era. Like Duneier (1992), I believe much of the literature about African Americans' life-world is systematically flawed with stereotypes and caricatures. Understanding the four men's life-world may thus require us to recognize how racist ideology impacted their lived experiences.

Even though we were denied our human rights, we were taught by our families to work hard, to dream, and to struggle for racial and community uplift. We thus learned values that prevented us from seeing ourselves as victims, or even as an oppressed or marginalized people. Mr. Leon recalls, for example, that "Our parents not only taught us a behavior for coping with racism, but they also prepared us to cope with racial prejudice outside of our community while still maintaining our sense of who we were." I, like most of my peer group, have despondently come to the conclusion that the kinds of Black families we knew back then no longer exist. Mr. Dwight observes, "Today's society has no controls over children that our community had when we were growing up."

Mr. Lee notes, " If you did something wrong back then, you had to answer not only to your family but also to your community, and if not, you had to leave the neighborhood and go north." Mr. Leon explains, "No one wanted to embarrass his/her family because if a family member did something wrong, the entire family would be viewed as criminals." Mr. Curtis adds, " Family and community controls were good for everyone, because they kept us out of many unseen difficulties. Without family and social controls what do you have? You have confusion, bewilderment, perplexity."

Back then, it was a psychological burden to accept traditional Black parental authority and expected social conduct for the four Black men. However, none of the men regrets this kind of family constraint. They tend to believe that such boundaries are very important if Black children are going to be successful and valuable to their community. Parental authority was established and preserved by physical punishment that thoroughly reminded us about respect for authority and for our community. Disrespecting others, unpleasant attitudes, and rudeness were unthinkable.

Mr. Lee notes, "You just did not talk back to your parents." I observed a few years ago an elderly Black lady carrying a very large wooden rod while walking a few steps ahead of her grandchildren. A younger Black woman gently asked the elderly Black lady why she was carrying that wooden rod. The elderly Black lady replied, while pointing toward the county deputy sheriff, "If I do not restrain them now, the policemen will do it." "That is the kind of nurturing we experienced," Mr. Lee says. Mr. Dwight observes, "Our parents taught us that if we were going to successful in the world, there were certain expected behaviors."

The four men and I cannot discern what impact family control had on young people' success. Furthermore, the word "success" may be an elusive and relative term for these men. Thus, I treat this term "success" in a postmodernist and qualitative framework. All the while I agree with the participants that parental authority plays an important role in developing character and preparing African American males to meet future challenges. The Black extended family is crucial in creating successful Black men then.

Despite trials and tribulations back then, Black families encouraged experiences of self-sufficiency and interdependence. Black families were painfully aware of the value of quality education. They instilled in their children that excellent education is the primary means of escaping crime and poverty (Tatum, 1987). The four men and I realize that at present African American young men have a greater chance of going to prison than going to college, are three times more likely to live in poverty or be killed by police, six times more likely to be killed on the streets, five times more likely to be arrested for robbery, and twice as likely to drop out of school (Gentry & Peelle, 1994). Racism, lack of parental involvement, hostile neighborhood, and negative self-image contribute to crime and deviant behavior among African American males (Billson, 1996).

The four men believe that early parental involvement was a key to their success. We all believe that this same kind of life-world is important to African American males today. Mr. Lee explains, "We cannot lay all of the blame on the White man for what many Black parents failed to do. Back then, our parents were intensely involved in our school activities as well as our after school activities. They knew where we were supposed to be at all times."

Based on my understanding of their narratives, I sense that these men's families were able to assess the world around them with a profundity and complexity that often goes unrecognized in modernist narratives. Their families were aware of stereotypical portrayals of young African-American men as alienated, angry, and violent (Young, 1996). However, they were not so frustrated or angry about the limited opportunities to fail to provide adequately for their children's future back then. Instead, like other parents, these parents commonly encouraged a positive self-image that permitted the four men to see themselves as extraordinary. As I listen to the four men's stories, I sense their families' sufferings, anguish and misery; at the same time, I sense the strength and confidence that their families instilled in them.

Some Black family members were responsible for providing a cultural identity to young Black men back then. Older family members prepared younger members to resist oppression. Although the four men were taught to put on an agreeable face around white people, they also heard the widely told narratives about Black families' experiences of exploitation and violence against them (Henderson,1999). They understood that Black families like their's clung to an inner strength perpetuated by extended kinship systems. Relying on this closeness, these men's families sustained a collective determination and a mindset of unity. Traditionally, this social arrangement has been the source of resilience for many African American males.

Paradoxically, many African American families lived in segregated neighborhoods marked by social and economic isolation. These Black families played a significant role in creating racial pride (Young, 1996). In order to survive emotionally and psychologically in early childhood, the four African American men learned constructive emotional responses toward racism. They grew up in homes where families promoted and expected productive behavior. Poverty within the African American families has been connected with immorality, violent behavior and felonies. However, the four men recall how they were nurtured during Jim Crow, despite their life-world of racial discrimination that violated their families' basic human rights and forced many Black families into poverty and deprivation.

They survived and lived to make a difference with their own families and in the Black community. The four African American men and their extended families found ways to create a sense of shared experiences of unity and caring despite racism, with its economic and educational obstructions (Freeman, 2004; cf. Meares, 2004). Perhaps Black families found a thousand different ways to survive, to cope with stigmatization, marginalization and racial discrimination back then. Perhaps during that era it was a protective shield for African American children. I cannot say what would have been these men's fate without this life-world of protectiveness.

Back then poverty was taken for granted; it defined the Black family's lived experiences in perverse ways. Part of my challenge is to examine the social structure of Black families that permitted these men to become successful back

59

then. Nowadays, poverty is different. It appears to be a distinct demarcation that severely restricts one's life chances. Racial prejudice and stereotypes imply that once African American families become poor, they are likely to stay poor; not so for these four Black men's families (Danziger & Lin, 2000). That may explain in part why the four men became successful (Wilson, 1990). Despite poverty, they had family prayer community closeness.

Back then, African American extended families were the ethical training grounds for young African American men. We did encounter the kind of problems within the Black families that we see today, such as divorce, single parents and incarcerations. Yet we had a collective consciousness and a thriving Black community strongly based on traditions of survival. It was a life-world where emotional and spiritual support were readily available to us. Our extended family was a self-contained sanctuary, where family gatherings were regular lived experiences. Family was typically a place of togetherness, closeness and affection. The Black family had survived years of suffering and appalling treatment, yet created a mindset of optimism for their children (Deotis, 1980).

The life-world of Black extended family gatherings back then cultivated unity and a sense of warmth. Within this family structure, African American males were able to feel valued in spite of racial oppression. Today individualism and affluence tend to have weakened extended family relationships (Deotis, 1980). Back then, though, the Black family created a surprisingly complicated set of survival skills and social mobility. By now it seems apparent that African Americans back then did not internalize the harmful images of themselves put forward by mainstream (Cross, 1978).

For example, from 1925 until 1970, the great majority of African American families were two-parent households embedded in a well-organized, cohesive, and supportive kinship system. This information means that up until the 1970's, persistent poverty did not have the detrimental effects on African American family socialization that are widely cited (Cross, 1978). The four men are alarmed and discouraged about the state of today's Black family. They observe that too many Black families have been turned over to welfare and social service agencies, instead of relying on the Black community.

Historically, not only were African American males cared for by their kin or fictive kin, but it was also common for neighbors to provide child care in their neighborhood. Extended Black family members including fictive kin such as special neighbors, have been caring for each other throughout their history in many informal ways (Chipungu, Everett & Leashore, 2004).

Black Community Now and Then

The four men painfully describe how their old neighborhoods have changed and now have gone from a once thriving community to deserted buildings and vacant lots. Mr. Curtis explains: how the Black community has gone from bad to worse, from a place called home to a battle zone of crime, recklessness and disobedience. Now it seems that the Black community is largely a place of broken spirits and empty lives (Deotis, 1980).

These and the following data emerge from the respondents' own words as

61

well as from historical data. The 1940's and the 1950's were difficult times for the Black community. Our poverty inspired resourcefulness, though, as we have seen. Mr. Lee points out, "White people have no idea what it is like to live in a racist society, to be Black and male and pressured to accept a stereotypical identity." Growing up, we drew on our community for motivation and aspirations. Back then, the burden of striving for success seems to have been less oppressive than it is for many African Americans today. We were family back then, we shared back then, we suffered and hungered back then. In short, we hoped back then. By and large, the four participants and I share these perceptions.

Ironically, the Black community was forced to unite for safety, survival and resistance. It may be unnecessary to further point out that community caring was vital to successful African-American males back then. Mr. Leon notes, " In many ways the Black community was the parents' eyes and ears to watch over you." We more or less had to become a self-contained retreat where family gatherings were a common ritual that provided an environment of togetherness, closeness, friendship and warmth.

When I was growing up back then, the Black community was also an enclave of liveliness and music. Its people were often energetic and full of life; the streets were crowded with motivated and involved people. Neighborhood unity, strength of mind, and role models were common. Mr. Dwight informs us that many individuals who lived in the Black community encouraged him to strive for better things in life, such as a good job, clothes, house and car. He refused to surrender his dream of having a better life than the earlier generation. He never thought about settling for less, and he understood well that he had to work hard and would have to make many sacrifices to realize his dreams.

Back then, as young African American males we had opportunities to learn from the older men within the Black community about survival and even thriving in a racist society. The African American community emphasized academic achievement and self-control. I later discovered that the four men were not guided by hegemonic Euro-American values and images to define their identity or life-world. Jim Crow laws and the Eurocentric views were ineffective in providing Black men with the model of action they adopted to realize their dreams (Crawley & Freeman, 1993).

On the other hand, community caring encouraged the four men to study harder, especially for teachers whom they liked and trusted. In the world of segregation, community caring was deliberate and collaborative (Snarey & Walker, 2004). Mr. Curtis observes, "No matter what one's education level was back then, we were just like everyone else in the community." I realized early on that no one in my community was treated any differently because of economic and social status. For example, Mr. Leon notes, "We valued the words of warnings from Joe the wino whenever he told us to stay out of trouble and go home." I recall that a number of African American men living in our Black segregated community were called Joe the wino. Generally, they were unemployed, high school dropouts who knew nearly everyone in the community and were aware of its questionable activities.

63

Back then, our Black community organizations also offered types of community control. Imbedded within these organizations were lessons learned and internalized. Perhaps, these social controls had a significant impact on the success of these men and myself, especially to the extent that controls were integrated into a larger social network. They seemed to have shaped the socialization process that helped African American males become aware of their opportunities in society. The *Black* Boy Scouts of America was one such organization. Back then, we were very proud when each of us became a member of that organization.

Mr. Dwight observes, "Our Black community organizations such as Boy Scouts of America kept us out of trouble" back then. "Our Boy Scout leaders were Black men who lived in our community." They knew us as individuals. They knew where we lived, and how well we were doing in school, and some of the men were schoolmates of our teachers. Mr. Dwight notes, "They even knew our church membership, the name of our ministers, as well as our extended family members."

Mr. Curtis adds, "Black scouts leaders were our mentors, and told us what to do and how to stay out of trouble." The Black Boy Scout organization within our community was our home away from home. It was a highly respected community organization where young lives were transformed, but not necessarily in the quantitative sense. You could see on our faces the sense of growth, becoming and belonging. Perhaps the path to success started there; I cannot tell. I am aware, though, how it inspired us to do our best.

Some of these leaders were school teachers, Sunday school teachers and our neighbors. The four men and I felt a sense of unity and belonging in that organization. We were very proud back then and felt important when wearing the Boy Scout uniform. It was not the organization itself that shaped our perspective, but rather its nurturing and intimacy. It also offered another social framework, another social border, and another protective enclosure. Mr. Curtis, as well as the other four men's lament, "Today, there is no *Black* Boy Scouts organization within the Black community. Our Black youths no longer have the kind of community connection and controls we had back then and know nothing about the kind of world we enjoyed."

Since the four men were socialized within a demoralizing, intimidating society that more or less infiltrated every aspect of their lives, they provide insights about navigating Jim Crow. I understand that our socialization process was from an Afrocentric standpoint that was essential for survival and allowed us to counter racism on our own terms, values and standards. While the men valued mainstream society, they did not commit psychological suicide by denying their Blackness. Their Afrocentric perspective was a lens that attuned them to their shared experiences. Their perspective seems to derive from an interactive process whereby the community structured their behavior and helped them internalize values of personal commitment as well as social and economic development within the Black community (Crawley & Freeman, 1993).

The Black community's organizations provided and encouraged healthy choices about whether the men would overcome or be overcome; whether they would cave in to the injustices or be transformed by transcending their oppression and living as whole individuals as much as possible in a broken society. It appears that the four men found vigorous and appropriate ways to express themselves in less threatening ways by balancing their manhood with compliance. Their attitudes were not reflective of the pathology, deviance, or inferiority mindset that is so often portrayed in the literature. All of the men viewed their community in extremely positive ways by citing examples of its closeness back then.

It appears that the four men had the ability to analyze, think through, and plan for their future, despite having to deal with Jim Crow, denied opportunities, and the prospect of crushed dreams. Mr. Curtis acknowledges that "My educational goals and achievement were merely ordinary." Mr. Leon notes, "It was not surprising, It was not until years later that I realized we were poor or disadvantaged. In our community, we had everything everyone else had in their community." He adds, "None of us were aware how poor in spirit, poor in caring and poor in unity were those who lived outside of our community."

If the four men had had all of the latest technology such as computers, cell phones and other telecommunication devices, I wonder where they might be today, and if they would have been as psychologically fortified back then. Mr. Curtis notes, "I believe we were blessed, cared for and had all of the things that were necessary for survival." Before racial integration the Black community created its own autonomy. Mr. Lee recalls, "We had our own Black clothing shops, furniture stores, restaurants, groceries stores, hair salons, fraternities, sororities, book clubs, social and private associations, as well as community-responsible associations." I recall that we even had our high society coalition of men and women who were deeply involved and connected to the Black community.

Black doctors and Black dentists were personally known throughout the Black community. Even though our Black community had been marginalized by mainstream society, it was autonomous. For many African-American males, integration and the Civil Rights laws were not especially beneficial, helpful or even profitable. For one reason, the Black community lost its unparalleled and historical distinctiveness. Mr. Leon recalls, "Back then there was no drug problem, high crime rate, or drive-by shootings. We were safe living in our community." Mr. Leon also recalls, " Once you entered the neighborhood you were safe, you were safe from police brutality, from name calling and from being stopped and searched *driving while Black*." At times, the four men emphasize more about what they did not experience rather than what they did experience.

Mr. Leon notes, "Although we faced Jim Crow, we were proud of our community and were always reminded that we had something to prove to White people." Mr. Dwight explains, "I still work harder to prove White people wrong, and I will continue to strive to prove them wrong." The four men believe that Jim Crow was incapable of stripping the Black community of its humanity, incapable of destroying its hopes, and incapable of undermining its unity. Contrary to the grand narratives that prevailed back then, the Black community did much better than what one might expect. It faced many obstacles, yet still maintained strong family relationships and a sense of community that functioned as an extended family. For the four Black men and others the Black community was an extended family

Back then, the Black community addressed its oppressive conditions as well as issues of political disempowerment and was aware of its responsibility to deal with social problems. The oppressed must deal with their dilemma themselves, or the oppressors will do it for them according to their own values and interests (Rocchio, 2000). In many ways the Black community encouraged racial pride, self-help, intellectual growth and self-determination (Rocchio).

As members of that world, the four men refused to accept the limitations and negative images of the Black community in mainstream society (Comer & Poussaint, 1992). Elsewhere, too, transcendence prevailed. For example, "The lives of Blacks in Charleston were hardscrabble, but racism and poverty inspired resourcefulness. There was a sense that the world owed you nothing, and even if it did, it wasn't going to pay up soon" (Brown, 1995). It is impossible to bring back the essence of the Black community back then. Perhaps, more research about the Black community back then could establish a relationship between racial identity and successful African American males. Yet, I am unsure whether we can apply the values endorsed by the Black community back then. Jim Crow required the Black community to become self-sufficient, close and cohesive in order to survive.

The Black community was a stimulating learning environment back then that prevented dysfunctional and psychological resignation. It also insulated us from many public insults (Armstrong, 1998). The four men have vivid memories of their life-world back then; it is one that is often relived through contacts with others who lived during the era of segregation.

The four men are aware of the effects of racism, poverty and African American males with low self-worth who unsurprisingly have gone astray (Cross, 1978). Mr. Leon laments, "The Black community socialization process that we experienced no longer exists today." One may argue that the Black community socialization process would not have the same effect on African-American males today as it did during the 1940's and the 1950's (Jones, 1979). Indeed, the plight of the African American males today may be the result of a psychological and social transformation within the Black community. Perhaps it is because we have experienced the loss of a collective consciousness and the loss of a close community based on shared experiences of oppression, domination and legal discrimination.

It was a time and place where no one locked their doors; it was also a time of shared hardships, but no one carried their burdens alone. Regretfully, times have changed; our Black community has changed. Our life-world of traditional survival skills guarded and guided us toward success. That seems to be all gone now. Young African American males will likely never know the kind of psychological support available to us back then.

Contrary to various stereotypical images, then, the Black community's milieu gave us a sense of purpose and a practical belief within ourselves that we could succeed in life if we worked hard and endured racism. Before the Civil Rights era, our lived experiences reinforced motives of self-determination. The

69

Black community back then allowed us to internalize a positive identity that provided a strong foundation for achievement. It was supposed back then that being a member of a legal and oppressive caste before integration had an unfavorable even destructive effect on us (Beteille, 2002). I believe the caste system encouraged the Black community back then to organize and to develop creative ways to survive.

I am incapable of telling the men's narratives about their once thriving Black community without permitting them to indirectly reminisce and allowing them to recollect their thoughts about a lost world of closeness. Racial integration for the four participants was the beginning of the end of a world they had known. Unexpectedly they have noticed that the concept of racial uplift vanished and a social and economic decline within the Black community. Despondently, they describe the conditions within the Black community today. Instead of places where Black children used play they see dirty faces, empty lots, junked cars, and crack houses; instead of seeing smiling faces, they see wretchedness and instead of fresh baked bread they smell toxic air and polluted water.

CHAPTER V

CONCLUSION

Education and Leadership

One of the privileged realities of growing up as an African American male

back then was that we were constantly instructed to rise above the horizon of

ordinariness. Back then, leadership within the Black community was exemplified

by informal interactions, and mere outward show was not allowed. Black leaders

commonly and persistently encouraged us to achieve to the utmost of our ability.

One function of African American leadership back then was to socialize African

American males to value education and their personal worth as well as to

understand racism and successfully fight oppression (Swadener & Lubeck, 1995).

Back then, when the four men and I were growing up, Black leaders were

highly respected within the community, often without regard to social or

educational status, and despite the number of teachers and church leaders assigned

those positions. Mr. Dwight notes, "Black leaders in the post-civil rights era were

moral and exceptional men who encouraged us to work toward success, but at

present, we have a Black leadership crisis within the Black community." Mr.

Curtis observes, "But times have changed now. There are so many different things

that can capture the hearts and minds of our Black youth."

Mr. Dwight also says, "There is a battle for the hearts and minds of young African American males, and a battle between the streets and Black leadership."

In many ways civil rights laws made it unproblematic for middle-class African Americans leaders to move out of segregated communities, even while many Blacks were left behind educationally and otherwise. This social change created a psychological chasm between Black leaders and educationally disadvantaged Blacks. Back then, there were no substantial social distinctions between Black leaders and those who were worse off except for levels of responsibility. We were told to work and to study hard in order to escape poverty, and at the same time we had Black leaders as role models.

Education

The four men identify what I believe may be intangible factors central to their success back then. Possibly, these factors were not a recipe for success in and of themselves. Perhaps, though, they were part of these men's life-world that ultimately shaped their achievement-oriented mindset. The four men feel that their uplifting was due in many cases to African American teachers. Loose lives had no place in the world of teachers who were to lead African American youths. Those Black men and women lived by example. They were spiritual, intellectual and psychological counselors and mentors who were better suited in many respects than some parents (Gates & Ronnick, 2006).

Mr. Lee notes, "You had no choice but to do well in school. Black teachers would often notify the parents of the respective students if they skipped school. Back then Black students could not easily skip school." He observes, "It seems that parents knew exactly where their children had been all day, even before they arrived home." Mr. Leon explains, "It was hell to pay if Black parents discovered their children had missed school." Going to school, then, was not a matter of choice for the four men. It was inescapable.

Mr. Curtis explains how he was motivated: "Black teachers expected and demanded all of us to learn and do extremely well in school. If they did not do well or were behaving badly in their classrooms, the teachers would pick up the phone and call their parents." Mr. Dwight recalls, "Black teachers talked as if it was the parents' responsibility to explain their children's behavior to them." Mr. Leon says, "During segregation we had brilliant teachers and principals who not only insisted on quality scholarship but character distinction as well." Back then, Black students saw their teachers as highly intelligent persons who demanded that we learn according to our ability. They were trying to get us to internalize outwardly acceptable behaviors that would allow White people to see us as non-threatening individuals. Furthermore, it was taken for granted that our appearance was conspicuously important.

To me as well as to the four men, our success seems to have depended on how we presented ourselves to White people. For example, not only in our classrooms but also in the school's cafeteria, we were scrutinized and often scolded for talking loudly or not sitting up straight. As part of our instruction, we learned to act differently around White people. Whenever White people visited our school, we often exhibited our finest behavior, at least until they left the school grounds. Our education thus included performing and meticulously conducting ourselves around White people. Learning this double standard was possibly essential to our survival.

While learning to fabricate and to demonstrate humility around Whites, we were allowed to unwind and be ourselves around other Blacks. We were learning to selectively speak and to act White as we learned the survival skill of social deception involving public compliance and superficial smiles. In many ways our segregated education entailed a socialization that revolved around the struggle to move into the middle class. We were taught that if we wanted to become successful, we had to assimilate and seek White people's acceptance. Yet by now no amount of school reform can reproduce the educational practices back then. The *Black pedagogy* we experienced served to counteract many of the negative consequences of educational inequality and psychological deprivation. Black teachers rejected any premise that we were inferior or were disadvantaged students or slow learners.

School integration cannot offer lived experiences of unity and the life-world of closeness that we knew back then. In our Black school we learned to act like intellectuals even though the school was less than satisfactory. Mr. Dwight explains, "We were not aware that our education was perceived as inferior." Besides, none of us knew that our curriculum was much different from that of the White schools. Unfortunately, I was extremely aware that our Black school was intellectually dreadful because of my previous three years of Catholic education. For me, enrolling in a Black high school was like going to an insane asylum or, less dramatically, a place without the high performance standards that I had known. Many Black parents, however, looked to the Black teachers for their children's economic and social liberation. I recall a number of instances when Black teachers became mentors of students back then, who often in turn became successful individuals.

I believe Black teachers' mentorship had some significant impact on the four men's accomplishments. For example, Mr. Lee recalls, "It was normal for Black teachers to inspire us by saying that we could accomplish anything that we set our minds to." I did not personally experience this inspiration from my Black teachers. Perhaps, as an ex-Catholic school student I was an outsider, or at least at times I sensed it. It was difficult for me to adjust to the Black public school system because my Catholic school teachers were academically demanding, caring White women. For me the Catholic school was a militaristic setting where learning, punishments and rewards were predictable as well as greatly challenging.

Despite those cherished early years, I do recall a number of times in high school when before classes and sometimes near the end of classes, Black teachers would remind us about the achievements of Black people. In their own ways, they challenged Whites' assumptions about our academic ability. At times, Black teachers would tell the four men and me about Black leaders. For example, "By 1902, it was demonstrated that we could learn by the fact that more than four hundred African American males received their bachelor's degree from Harvard, Yale, Oberlin, and seventy other top universities" (DuBois,1970).

Black teachers back then created an educational setting that allowed us to define ourselves in ways that undermined White people's commonplace expectations. We learned, then, both to accommodate their expectations in appearance and demeanor and to overcome them in our work as well as in our own community. Black teachers thus placed great importance on quality education and realized its social and economic value.

By and large, they persuaded us that we could live productive and successful lives (Mincy, 1994). Many of our Black teachers used their own life experiences as models for teaching us both how to overcome racism and how to act in the White world. Some would argue that our Black teachers taught us to accept and adjust to an oppressive social system. Those Black teachers who recognized the racist power structure and openly demonstrated their loyalty to the White establishment were in many ways, though, the only ones among us able to keep their jobs and fight educational disparities. As Mr. Dwight points out, "Black teachers were the guardians of our educational system, however fearful to openly participate in changing the system."

Segregation also promoted interarical networking that seems sometimes to have made success more likely. School sports are illustrative. Athletic coaches were also among our mentors. They helped to motivate us and kept us on track academically. Mr. Curtis illustrates below.

> I was fortunate because the coaches were very interested in our grades and our personal lives. You had to get your schoolwork first of all. We also had to provide a progress school report in order to continue to play sports; our grades had to be at a certain grade level. If you did not have a

76

certain grade, you could not play. The coaches were not only our coaches for a certain time during the day, but they were our mentors and were well respected people we knew within the Black community as well. Most Black teachers knew our parents on some level, so it was not strange to discover that the coaches also knew the parents of their students.

For our competitive athletics had to go outside of our school district. Mr. Dwight explains, "We had limited schools that you could compete with. Black schools could only compete with Black schools back then because it was unlawful." I recall that our own Black school had a basketball and a football team that competed with other Black schools in Atmore, Mobile, and Birmingham, Alabama, as well as in Tallahassee, Panama City, Jacksonville, and Miami, Florida. Black teachers, family members, and others from the Black community regularly traveled to such cities to see the games. Mr. Dwight notes

These Black schools created a social network that few realized at that time. Black teachers, school principals and family members became aware of each school's academic achievements. Black teachers got to know other Black teachers from the respective cities. They allied themselves toward racial uplift and developed racial pride in their respective Black schools. Before and after each game, visiting teachers would tour the respective schools and the surrounding neighborhoods. Regularly there were banquets and dances for the visitors and the respective team members. The opposing teams members would dine together and talked about the game experiences as well as about their goals in life. Because of these social events, Black principals and teachers got to know each and shared how well their respective students were doing in school.

Perhaps this phenomenon influenced our character; I am unsure. I do believe these events had a positive influence on our attitudes about success. For many of us, it was not an astonishing or surprising thing to see many of these team members (football and basketball) go on to play professional sports. Possibly, our life-world of school and extracurricular activities is unparalleled.

Many of our teachers challenged us to go to college yet for many of us the first year of college was a discouraging experience. Mr. Lee recalls,

It was not until I arrived at a Black college that I realized I was not as prepared for college as I could or should have been. Going to college was great learning experience and an amazing opportunity to be there. I will never forget the kind of assistance that I received that enabled me to learn on the college level.

We all were familiar with this lived experience of academic frustration as well as assistance from Black teachers. I also discovered that many professors had internalized the same commitment to racial uplift that we had experienced in high school. These college instructors were determined to teach, inspire and encourage Black students to do well in life. We were just as determined to meet their expectations.

To grasp further their notions about schooling and success, I asked the four participants about today's schools. Mr. Lee says, "Today Black parents and teachers don't get involved with their children like our parents did years ago."

Mr. Dwight explains, "I see very little of Black teachers getting personally involved with Black students like they did back then." Mr. Curtis laments today's educational circumstances for Black students, "Black students are mostly taught by White teachers who do not share collective experiences of racial uplift." Mr. Leon says, for example, "Today Black students, and especially Black males, are being vilified, discredited and stigmatized by White teachers, and consequently Black students do not study and strive as hard in school as they ought to."

Mr. Dwight says, "School integration was very harmful for Black students in many respects. There was a time when we had our Black segregated schools. It was a time when all Black teachers expected their Black students to academically achieve."

Back then, it does appear Black school teachers generally worked with parents to identify and address the needs of African American male students (Levin, 1970). Mr. Dwight notes

Today many Black students appear to have no value in education, and no one in their family seems to value education like we did back then. In those days, your teachers and family all came together to make sure you did what you were supposed to do. Today I try to show the kids that instead of being a part of a second or third generation of a welfare system, I try to get them to tell me the thing that they like to do in life.

Mr. Curtis observes, "Today most teachers are White and strangers. They do not go in the same circles, do not attend the same churches, do not have the same kind of communication and do not have the interest in our Black students that once existed." Mr. Curtis alludes to how Black segregated schools were firmly rooted in the Black community: "I personally knew my school principals, the assistant principals and teachers. We went to the same barbershops and Black stores, and I also knew Black doctors and Black dentists." Mr. Dwight laments, "Our school curriculum is now controlled by White superintendents, principals and interest groups who see no value or place for Black students or their history."

I sense the four men assume that most Black students cannot move into the mainstream lacking a quality education as well as racial pride. While I knew these men appreciate their Black segregated schools and Black heritage as elements of their success, they also understand that an inferior education back then was an intellectual and psychological impediment for many Black students. None of the men suggests a return to segregated schools or even recreating separate institutions. Instead, they want control of Black neighborhood schools to ensure that Black students receive not the kind of education that they received but a high-quality, community-based education.

Mr. Lee laments, "Thrusting Black students into predominantly White classrooms does little or nothing to enhance their education. Racism in our schools may take away all learning incentives and creates an educational environment that dampens African-American students' ability to learn." Mr. Dwight observes, "There appears to be a disconnect between our upbringing and those of Black students today. We were encouraged to do the best we could, but today I do not see this optimistic attitude in our Black students."

Today, as back then, our Black community requires teachers who are prepared to labor and devote themselves to students. Black teachers back then had family and community ties that created commitment and openness toward most of their students. The Black school's milieu was a life-world of familiarity and encouragement. It was ordinary to see Black parents visit their children's homeroom teachers without an appointment and without seeing the principal. Mr. Dwight observes, "You really got a positive feeling going to school." Mr. Leon also notes, "We respected our teachers a great deal. They had few discipline problems back then in comparison to what we see today." We all agree that we need to renew these circumstances.

Mr. Lee explains, " Our teachers cared for us and believed all of us could learn." Mr. Curtis notes, "Today too many teachers come to school with their minds made up that Black students cannot learn." Back then our classrooms offered some students lived experiences of self-realization. In some ways, our Black teachers used their teaching position as a social and political stage to educate us about how to act and survive and achieve in a White world. Their rules and expectations made fierce demands on us. Yet, they were persistent and adamant in teaching us about the realities of social norms and racial politics.

The four African American men experienced a sense of community closeness Within the school setting. Their narratives of self-determination offer inspiration as well as an appreciation of the history of Black education. Highly successful Black schools back then had strong neighborhood relationships, helped to give the Black community its identity, and encouraged parents' involvement. In turn, these schools nurtured successful men like the four participants in this study.

Leadership

Historically Black leaders played important roles in racial uplift notwithstanding their diversity of opinions and other differences. Back then, the most prevalent theme was racial uplift. But during the 1950's and early 1960's, Black leaders' worldviews began to undergo an extraordinary transformation (Ibarra & Lineback, 2005). Previously they had seldom asserted themselves publicly. But a new leadership phenomenon emerged. Before, Black leadership was characterized as racial uplift but now it is known as Civil Rights leadership. "Racial uplift" and "lift as we climb" gave way to individualism intertwined with social politics. All the while, the life-world the four men and I had known was slowly disappearing, leading us to ponder the future of Black leaders who had sustained and supported us through slavery and Jim Crow and into the Civil Rights era. Black leaders had heightened our awareness of resistance, survival and race improvement.

Today it appears that a chasm has materialized between Black leadership and the Black community. The communal contacts of Black leaders back then that once reinforced the four men's collective consciousness and shared lived experiences of mutual respect have virtually disappeared. This gulf has created a social dilemma for many of today's Black youths. Perhaps they feel further disconnected and isolated within as well as beyond their community and thus show signs of indifference. Possibly, they feel alone in the world and are left to fight their own battles as best they can against incredible odds (Ibarra & Lineback, 2005). Back then, when the four men and I were growing up, Black leadership took on a personal and community role.

The four men and I remember our Black leaders back then. They influenced our thinking about success. We identified with the intellectual abilities, support and faithfulness of Black leaders. Their example helped sustain us through difficult times, sometimes in invisible and subtle ways but perhaps serving as a means of our survival. Back then, as Mr. Curtis puts it, "Black leaders were highly regarded by Whites as respectable individuals." We were legally and socially stigmatized, but kept believing in Black leadership and its spiritual aspects that continue to influence us today. Our Black leaders created hope and a resolve to endure (Ibarra & Lineback, 2005). Consequently, Black people are still enduring.

Back then, Black leaders commonly advocated Blacks helping themselves as the main vehicle to racial advancement. Part of our history as Black people is making something out of nothing and finding a way out of no way. Historically, then, Black pride and Black leadership rested on faith in Black people to prosper in a racist society (Gates & Ronnick, 2006). As Mr. Leon puts it, "We clothed ourselves with reputable behavior and self-worth." Even though African American men were and still are classified as inferior because of their race, gender, and historically low social class, even at the height of Jim Crow they never stopped believing that racial uplift could improve their lives and the lives of other Black people (Stewart, 1997). Thus, the four African American men kept the faith in racial uplift.

Black leaders today must help strip away what is unproductive and superficial and expose those who pretend to be proponents of racial uplift. Perhaps Black leadership today is a thin covering for individuals who are using self-important titles, fancy vocabulary, powerful rhetoric, and inflated confidence to exert influence in the Black community (Gates & Ronnick, 2006).

Because of its pragmatism, back then Black leadership entailed encouragement that inspired a sense of pride. Day to day informal contacts stimulated higher ambitions among Black youths back then. These informal acquaintances were far more powerful influences than one might have supposed (Gates & Ronnick, 2006). Mr. Lee acknowledges, "Caring and closeness were taken for granted." Despite the number of well-meaning Black organizations today, they cannot recreate that kind of life-world we experienced. It appears that these organizations are unable to effectively address the needs of today's Black youth. Mr. Curtis asserts, "Black leaders seems to be running away from the real problems: neglect, hunger, lack of attention, love and closeness." I sense many Black leaders today do not personally know the lived experiences of poverty and hopelessness of the young Black men they are mentoring. These leaders tend to consist of middle-class educated Black men who do not hear nightly gun shots or the daily sounds of ambulances, it seems.

Mr. Dwight recalls, "Black leaders back then lived in our community and were personally in daily activities of survival, racial uplift and character

84

development." For example, the four men and I developed close relations with our Boy Scout leaders, church deacons, school teachers, and athletic coaches who knew our extended family members and teachers. Mr. Leon explains, "Black leaders were informal mentors, lived in our community and influenced our actions by warnings, advising and encouraging. Often, it didn't take much more than that."

Black leaders played significant roles in our lives back then. The Black Little League football and baseball coaches who managed teams often had no college degrees, yet they volunteered their time, instructed us in sports, and told us that we could do many things in life if we worked hard. Before and after practices they would talk to us about staying in school and doing our best. Looking back, I see our leaders' words offered wisdom to live by. These men were not great orators or educationally shrewd, but they encouraged us to focus on our future. Mr. Curtis notes, "Black leaders warmly talked about ideas with our parents. We instinctively knew that they cared about our future and wanted us to succeed." After we entered high school Black leaders inquired how we were doing and whether we were staying out of trouble.

To know these four men is to know their narratives, especially the trials and turning points that tested them and how they prevailed (Ibarra & Lineback, 2005). As a researcher and friend, I wanted to ensure my analysis fits with their lived experiences because I deeply identified with their narratives and how they make sense of the world. Like other narratives, theirs can offer comfort. While I encouraged the four men to express their views about Black leaders in their own language and consciously tried to leave lots of room for their voices, I instinctively noted how they cloaked their feelings, including possible bitterness, in ambiguous language. I supposed their silence and awkward moments involved anxieties about speaking openly. In their struggle for quality education, social justice, and liberation, these men depended profoundly on Black leadership.

Many Black leaders we knew back then remain unknown today. They were nevertheless powerful models of success, despite the fact that during Jim Crow their attitudes about the White world remained largely unexpressed. Their primary objectives were survival and caring for their families, not building a reputation. The four men recognize that things have changed now, and they believe that many Black leaders have forgotten racial uplift, and resigned themselves to racial inequality.

Perhaps, we as a people have changed. Back then, Black leaders developed a pedagogy and praxis that was historically framed for self-determination. I wonder whether Dr. King lived would he now be regarded as a traitor, an old man behind the times or an Uncle Tom. It appears that Black leaders today are looking for governmental assistance to solve our family and community problems. The four men do not oppose government programs for the poor, but they do believe that some programs tend to discourage personal responsibilities and economic freedom. Black leaders back then moved us toward self-reliance.

The old Black leaders that the four men and I knew are largely gone. Faith in God was a shared experience that united them back then. Although Jim Crow was oppressive, Black leaders kept our hopes alive. Their faith strengthened us through hunger, brutality, racism, lynching, and unfilled promises (Gill, 2000). They kept the torch of upward mobility and racial uplift burning intensely, notwithstanding the stereotypical images they endured as kowtowing, ignorant, subservient and afraid. The responsibility of today's Black leaders is to guide the next generation of young Black men (Gates and Ronnick, 2006).

We are aware of various Black leaders' voices, some seeming to hustle their theories that poor Black people are not trying hard enough to be successful. A few Black leaders have psychologically identified with White dreams, White living and White relationships.

Many Black leaders have been assimilated, and express little interest in conflicts beyond the African American community (Ray, 1971).

Mr. Lee notes, "The problem today is Black leaders are not self-reliant individuals like the men we knew back then." Mr. Curtis explains, "Black leaders risked their social and economic status in order to become responsible leaders. Some Black leaders even lost their employment when they spoke too loudly or forceful against racial discrimination back then." Mr. Leon observes," Silence on the part of Black leaders isn't going to get things done, ignoring the problem of inner-city isn't going to get things done and clinging to the old ways isn't going to get things done either."

Black leaders back then stressed future opportunities for African Americans while they personally struggled for their own survival. Although the methods of racial uplift were highly effective back then, Black leaders today must move beyond the pre-Civil Rights problem-solving era. It is necessary to construct a postmodernist paradigm that will provide new ways of thinking for the most marginalized and the most stigmatized within and beyond our community. Hope in a better future has been the cornerstone of Black leaders. Perhaps this pedagogy is even more crucial today. The modernist grounds for hope need to be replaced. But instead of replacing our modernist spirituals, we need to look in addition at postmodernist hip-hop as well. No less a social philosopher than Cornel West has done this (Stewart, 1997).

In order to further appreciate how Black leaders influenced the four men and me back then, it is helpful to talk about spirituals. The history of Black spirituals is a modernist narrative of a people subjected to terror, racism and oppression (Stewart, 1997). Living under oppressive conditions led Black leaders to sing the blues and "moan spirituals" such as *Sometime I Feel Like a Moaning Dove* and *Nobody Knows the Trouble I Sees* (Frazier, 1966).

Some older Black people favored the moaning preachers over the more sophisticated, rational, and intellectual ones because the moaning preachers helped them to define, articulate and confirm their anguish. Despite our Black leaders' differences, spirituals, both modernist and postmodernist, may assist many to overcome the sense of powerlessness. Through spirituals we can overcome the sense of being alone in the world. Spirituals may be crucial for psychological and spiritual healing.

Even after the Civil Rights era, Black leaders did not give up their mourning work. Instead, they established spirituals in contemporary American culture and beyond (Martin, A. & J. Martin, 1995). Their spirituals throughout the 20th century were among the resources that inspired Black leaders to establish Sunday schools, religious day schools, private religious academies, secondary schools, seminaries and institutions of higher learning (Franklin, 2004). They may thus lie among the preconditions for effective Black leaders as well as the Black church today.

CHAPTER VI

DISCUSSION

The four African American men's narratives have to a degree reflected the 1940's, and the late 1950's. It was a time of immense confusion about the life-world of Black people as researchers were unearthing the historical meanings of Whiteness and race relations. It was a time when White supremacy was religiously practiced, and when Black people were not allowed to use the city library. I would like to take a moment to highlight this life-world of the four men, coming of age in the Deep South. Their life-world and lived experiences back then are the underpinning of my dissertation. Back then, there were no Civil Rights laws, day care services, Food Stamps, free or reduced school lunches or fair housings laws. There were no equal employment laws or other measures such as affirmative action.

It was a time when daily newspapers printed stereotypical images of Black people; when deteriorating and dilapidated Black schools were the norm; when radio, television, and movies depicted Black people as stupid, lazy, dangerous, childish, and impractical. Back then, there were no sit-ins, marches, protests, or demonstrations, but we did pray. We prayed for better days and a time when we

90

would be judged not according to the color of our skin, but according to our character. We prayed for an opportunity to prove society wrong and to demonstrate our faithfulness. We prayed for White people to realize that we too are human beings and deserve to be treated like fellow citizens.

Despite their life-world of racial discrimination the men's narratives are not about victimitization or dreams deferred. At times evasive, these men did not portray themselves as wounded storytellers. They were appreciative of kind words of encouragement and the smiles of strangers. The came of age in a time when Blackness meant sharing, giving and caring and also a time of forgiving and looking further than our parents and grandparents had. It was a time of racial uplift, becoming, growing and rising. In many ways, the four men and I lament the loss of those days back then, but we still sense an obligation to lift as we continue climbing.

I thought about a number of possible factors that may have helped us constructively face overt racism, school segregation, and inequality of opportunity. Many of the four men's responses appear to express an implicit pedagogy of liberation. While researching archival and scholarly literature appropriate for my study, I discovered an exemplary African American male who prevailed in astonishing ways. Perhaps revisiting his life-world will help us to understand the four men's lived experiences and outcomes.

William Sander Scarborough's (see pages 1-14) accomplishments are reflective of self-determination. The four men and I recall how the older Black generation collectively laid the groundwork for racial uplift, which entailed great sacrifices in view of their and limited resources. Paradoxically, perhaps, the prohibition of literacy in the slave code had a great deal to do with their determination to learn. This prohibition alone did not motivate former slaves to pursue learning but did become central to African Americans' definitions of freedom, progress, success, self-identity, and views about citizenship (Span, 2002).

Education for us back then was more than a means of personal and professional improvement; it was viewed as a foundation for achieving social and economic equality. Racism reinforced the belief that being educated was one of several essential strategies for dealing with Jim Crow. Black leaders including educators, understood back then that education would be central to both for social mobility and racial uplift (Span, 2002).

Thus, as we have seen, instead of accepting the status quo of Jim Crow back then, African Americans organized schools and educated themselves. Quality education was esteemed as an invaluable resource. It was so significant back then that many Black educators established private schools through their own efforts or with the help of others. More generally, Black people have often created systems of self-help and grassroots schools for themselves and their families.

Rising and Racial Uplift

Back then, we knew our teachers. They were our Sunday school teachers, neighbors, and friends. Many of them did everything in their power and often went beyond their duty to keep us in school. They also encouraged us to hope and inspired us toward higher goals. We had a greater appreciation for each other back then. We did not experience the kind of snobbishness, self-importance, deception, treachery, and betrayal within the Black community that we sometimes see now. Our word was our bond back then. It was all we had. Keeping our word was an expression of character.

Despite African Americans' self-determination, in order to survive and prosper in the White world, often we covered or hid our true selves behind masks whenever we came into contact with White people. Back then, Blacks were trained well in wearing their masks. Our masks were functional and essential if we wanted White people's approval. Ultimately, our masks became more valuable as we climbed the ladder of success (Cross, 1978). Although African Americans' pedagogy of racial uplift was the foundation of our economic and social progress, social stereotypes continue to define Blacks as inferior. We have practically no reliable protection against the stigmatic character culturally assigned to us.

Labeling and discrediting us from mainstream academic world evoked an unspoken determination that stigmas would not claim our minds, hands and hearts. Yet, despite considerable social and economic progress, racial integration materialized as a hollow dream and unfilled expectations. Consequently, many of us see that opportunities knocked quietly or not at all. For privileged White people, though, opportunities knocked repeatedly and loudly (Johnson, 2005).

Historically, the life-world and lived experiences of the four Black men are not that unusual. As we saw, our schools back then created a culture and a

93

tradition that nurtured positive educational outcomes. Effective Black teachers and community leaders stressed racial uplift, collective decision-making and collaboration with colleagues and parents within the Black community.

By contrast, today many African American men believe they can do little to change their plight. No matter what they do, no matter what they achieve and no matter who they are, they often believe White people will never accept them. Often experiencing hostility wherever they go, Black men begin to lose their capacity to discern authentic harm from imaginary injury (Rosenberg, 1966). At the same time, successful socialization of African American males may be seen as a transformation of their authentic Blackness (Bobo, Hudley & Michel, 2004).

It will take an awful lot on our part to turn these ashes of our time into beauty. I do not know what these ashes look like in Africa, Asia, or even in inner-city American slums, but I do know what they look like in my neighborhood. We must get beauty out of these ashes by educating African American males and turning their sorrow into joy. We must go beyond catchphrases and beyond earlier racial uplift. To see, to walk, and to hear, but to do so without promise, without purpose, without direction, and without hope is plainly more of the same. Hope is the most powerful weapon on earth, and it has sustained African Americans through years of racial oppression, lynching and imprisonment. Hope for African Americans is more indispensable today than ever before. Nothing less will do, for hope is all we know and all we have (Conference for Urban Ministers, 1987). It is a hope that is beyond knowing.

I learned all of this and far more from the four participants. I became progressively aware that simply experiencing a group's life-world even as an insider, does not automatically make me an authority concerning it. To study one's lived reality requires a removal of self and a fresh kind of perspective about that reality that leaves the researcher's lived experiences on the border between that life-world and some other life-world (Anderson & Zuberi, 2000). It may require critical thinking and creative thoughts for explaining the phenomenon, as well as identifying hidden and invisible contradictions. Perhaps then the researcher can discern what is really going on beneath the surface of a life-world.

Another Bridge To Cross

Forty-three years ago Selma, Alabama became a famous place in American history. What happened on the Edmund Pettus Bridge illustrated the ruthlessness of many white people's attempt to maintain oppression and inequality. On that day Blacks were resolved not to bypass the bridge of self-determination. African Americans' long march to freedom met a blockade of brutal confrontation by law enforcement officers. On that bloody Sunday, more than 600 African American marchers strode forward with remarkable calmness, putting their lives on the line for their human rights, including above all the right to vote. They encountered brutality, police dogs and water hoses. Lives were lost.

Today there are other bridges to cross. As long as there are substandard inner-city schools for African American males, there is a bridge to cross. As long as there are social and economic injustices, there is a bridge to cross. As long as African Americans are allowed to grow up in poverty and in hunger, there is a

95

bridge to cross. As long as some White teachers are unwilling or unable to teach African American students to read and write, there is a bridge to cross. As long as African Americans are marginalized, oppressed and stereotyped as deviants, there is a bridge to cross. Finally, there is yet another bridge to cross. It is a bridge as challenging and daunting as all the others. The last bridge is one to empowerment, critical thinking, and social justice for all people (Cox, M. & Associates, 2005).

To cross this last big bridge as well as the other bridges requires an inclusive, pluralistic consciousness of history, culture, and social structure. It requires knowing in detail that African Americans contributions are unparalleled, not only out of slavery and destitution but also out of illiteracy, non-citizenship, and illegitimacy. No other people have accomplished more under parallel circumstances. No valid history of the United States can disregard African Americans' part in building this country to what it is today (Bell, 1923). Yet race has been and remains a major determinant of African Americans' life chances. The preponderance of race as a prime factor in the life-world of Blacks means that Blacks and Whites continue to live in two separate worlds that are still largely taken for granted as unequal and valid right up to this present day (Allen, Brown & Dawson, 1989).

There is no simple walk to self-determination anywhere, and many of us will have to pass through the valley of the shadow of death over and over again before we reach the mountain tops of our dreams. Dangers and difficulties have not discouraged us in the past, and they will not terrify or even impede us now. But we must be equipped to struggle as our forerunners did, wasting no time in unproductive talk and redundant action. We must, for instance, announce our firm

belief that everyone has the right to quality education and self-determination.

Education should promote the full development of human character and

strengthen respect for human rights and basic freedom. Our plight as Black people

compels resistance to the foul policies of inequality that prevail in this country.

Back then we understood the long struggle, contradictions, and opposition

bordering our community, but our neighborhood was safe. It was a life-world of

togetherness, intimacy, and a shared ideology; it was a place of unlocked doors

and windows, where we slept on front porches with family, friends and neighbors.

It was a place of family relationships, and a mindfulness that one day,

freedom would no longer be a dream deferred. Yet, the feelings and purpose of

the oppressed need not be vindictive. Like Nelson Mandela (1963), I have not the

least doubt that this dream will prevail. To bring this dissertation to a close while

reinforcing its findings about back then and right now, I offer the following poetic

transcription, consisting of words extracted from the four men's interview

transcripts.

At one time,

We were just plain_____Old colored folks

To just plain colored

We went from Black to Blue

To all shades of colors_____and all shades of hue

We went from Negro to Black_____To just plain Black

To Black is beautiful

With our Afros_____

We went from Sambo or Mammy _____Without a name

To selling our souls_____ to playing the game

We went from slavery to uncle Toms

From blackface_____ to pretend

Preferring to be white_____ while we grin

We went from African to Maroon

To Quadroon to Creole_____ and couldn't fit in

Yet,

We placed our hopes_____ Therein.

We went from passing for White_____Dreaming to be free

While our brothers were Dying_____

From that same oak tree!

REFERENCES

Aaron, V. (1999). The extended family as a source of support among African-Americans. *Challenge, 10*, 23-36.

Allen, L. R., Brown, E. R., & Dawson, C. M. (1989). A schema-based approach to modeling an African-American racial belief system. *American Political Science Review, 6* (83), 2.

Alloway, N. D., & Cordasco, F. (1970). *Minorities and the American city; a sociological primer for educators*. New York. McKay.

American Evaluation Association (2000). The prose and cons of poetic representation in evaluation reporting. *American Journal of Evaluation, 21*(3) Retrieved May 7, 2007, from http://research.uvsc.edu/mcdonald/ wanderweb/poetic_transcription.htm. Amos, R.T.

Anderson, E., Zuberi, T. (2000). The study of African American problem: W. E. B. Du bois's agenda, then and now. *The Annals of the American Academy of Political and Social Science, 568*.

Andrews, D. P. (2002). *Practical theology for the black churches: Bridging Black theology and African American folk religion*. Louisville, KY. Westminster.

Armstrong, T. (1998). *Awakening genius in the classroom*. Alexandria, VA:

Association for Supervision and Curriculum Development.

Asumah, N. S., & Perkins, C. V. (2001). *Educating the black child in the black*

independent schools. Binghamton, NY: Global.

Banks. I. W.(1987). *The vanishing Black family: Myth or reality?* A paper

presented at the Annual Meeting of the National Conference on the Black

Family in America 14th, Louisville, KY: Retrieved March 12, 2005, from

http://newfirstderarch.oclc.org/WebZ/FSFETCH?fetchtype

=fullrecord:sessionid-sp07sw05 p.12.

Barnes, S. (2003). Determinants of individual neighborhood ties and social

resources in poor urban neighbors. *Sociological Spectrum, 23,* 2.

Bell, J. (1923). The teaching of Negro history. *The Journal of Negro History,*

4 (7), 2.

Bell, J., Berger, T. M., & Feldman, S. M. (2003). Gaining access: A practical and

theoretical guide for qualitative researchers. New York. Altamira.

Berson, K. R. (1994). Marching to a different drummer: Unrecognized heroes of

American history. London: Greenwood.

Beteille, A. (2002). *Equality and universality: Essays in social and political*

theory. New Delhi: Oxford University.

Biber, N. S., & Leavy, P. (2004). *Approaches to qualitative research: A reader*

on theory and practice. New York. Oxford University.

Billson, J. (1996). *Pathways to manhood: Young Black males struggle for identity.* New Brunswick, NJ: Transaction.

Billings, G. L. (1992). Laboratory consequences of literacy: A case of culturally relevant instruction for African American students. *The Journal of Negro Education. 61*, 3.

Blackwell, E .J. (1991) The Black community: Diversity and unity. New York. Harper Collins.

Books, H.L., & Franklin, P.V. (1984). *Black self-determination: A cultural history of African American resistance.* Brooklyn, NY: Lawrence Hill Books.

Bobo, J., Hudley, C., & Michel, C. (2004*). The Black studies reader.* New York. Routledge.

Bright, J.A. (1994). Beliefs in action: Family contributions to African American student success. *Equity and Choice, 10,* 5-13.

Brown, T. (1995). *Black lies, the truth according to Tony Brown.* New York. Quill William Morrow.

Brooks, C. G., & Sedlacek, E.W. (1976). *Racism in American education: a model for change.* Chicago, IL: Nelson-Hall.

Bulter, S. J. (1998). Black America's true heroes. *The American Enterprise, 9,* 67-8.

Campbell, J. T. (1998). *Songs of zion: The African Methodist Episcopal church in the United States.* London: University of North Carolina.

Carr, M. J. (2003). Poetic expression of vigilance. *Qualitative Health Research. 13,* 9.

Chipungu, S. P., Everett, J. E., & Leashore, B. R. (2004). *Child welfare revisited: An africocentric perspective.* London: Rutgers University.

Coleman, A. B, & Shaw, K. M. (2002). Humble on sundays: Family, friends, and faculty in the upward mobility experiences of African American females. *Anthropology & Education Quarterly, 31,* 449-70.

College, D., Georgia, D., & Gibson, J. (1992). *Teachers are tracked, too. Tracked for failure/ tracked for success: An action packet to derail the negative effects of ability grouping. Task Force on Grouping and Tracking.* National Council of Teachers of English. Urbana, IL.

Collins, P. H. (2000). *Black feminist thought: Knowledge, consciousness, and the politics of empowerment.* New York. Routledge.

Comer, P. J., & Poussaint, F. A. (1992). *Raising Black children: Two leading psychiatrists confront the educational, social, and emotional problems facing black children.* New York. Plume.

Conference for Urban Ministers (1987). *The disadvantaged among the disadvantaged: Responsibility of the Black churches to the underclass, October 23-25, 1987; a conference for urban ministers, seminarians, public policy makers, denominational personnel, human service professionals, and others who work in or with the black community.* Cambridge, MA: Harvard Divinity School.

Cornelius, D. J. (1991). *When I can read my title clear: Literacy, slavery and religion in the antebellum south.* Columbia, SC: University of South Carolina.

Cose, E. (2002). *The envy of the world: On being a Black man in america.* New York. Washington Square.

Costen, M. (2001). African American spirituals. *Journal of Religious & Theological Information, 4,* 59-87.

Cox, M., & Associates (2005). *The pictorial world of the child.* New York. Cambridge University.

Crawley, B., & Freeman, E. M. (1993). Theme in the life views of older and younger African American males. *Journal of African American Studies, 1,* 15-29.

Cross, E.W. (1978). Black family and Black identity: A literature review. *The Western Journal of Black Studies, 2* (2), 111-24.

Danziger, S., & Lin, C. A. (2000). *Coping with poverty: The social contexts of neighborhood, work, and family in the African American community.* Ann Arbor, MI: University of Michigan.

Davidson, H. H., & Greenberg, J.W. (1967). *Traits of school achievers from a deprived background.* New York. City College of the City University of New York.

Denzin, K. N., & Lincoln, S.Y. (2003). *Strategies of qualitative inquiry.* Thousands Oaks, CA: Sage.

Deotis, R. (1980). *Roots of a Black future: Family and church.* Philadelphia: Westminster.

Dickerson, J. D. (2004).*The end of Blackness: Returning the souls of Black folk to their rightful owners.* New York. Pantheon Books.

103

Dubois, W. E. B. (1970). *The gift of Black folks: The Negroes in the making of America.* New York. Square Press.

Duneier, M. (1992). *Slim' table: Race, respectability and masculinity.* London: University of Chicago.

Evahn, C., Kratzer, L., & Mc Call, B. R. (1992). *High school underachiever.* Newbury Park, CA: Sage.

Fairclough, A. (2007). *A class of their own: Black teachers in the segregated South.* London: Harvard University.

Frank, A. W. (1995). *The wounded storyteller: Body, illness, and ethics.* Chicago, IL: University of Chicago.

Franklin, P. V. (2004). *Cultural capital and Black education: African American communities and the funding of black schooling, 1865 to the present.* Greenwich, CT: Information Age.

Frate, D. A., Shimkin, D. B., & Skimkin, E. M. (1978). *The extended family in Black societies.* Chicago, IL: Mouton.

Frazier, F. (1966). *The Negro family in the United States.* Chicago, IL: University of Chicago.

Freeman, E. (2004).*Reconceptualizing the strengths and common heritage of black families.* Springfield, IL: Charles C. Thomas.

Freire, P. (1970). *Pedagogy of the oppressed.* New York. Herder and Herder.

Gates, L. H., & Ronnick, V.M. (2006). *The works of William Sanders Scarborough: Black classicist and race leader.* Oxford: University.

Gentry, A. A., & Peelle, C. C. (1994). *Learning to survive: Black youth look for education and hope*. London: Auburn House.

Gill, M. L. (2000). *Daughters of dignity: African women in the bible and the virtues of black womanhood.* Cleveland, OH: Pilgrim.

Ginwright, S. A. (2002). Classed out: The challenges of social classes in Black community change. *Social Problems, 49*, 544-62.

Giroux, A. H. (1992) *Border crossings: Cultural workers and the politics of education.* New York. Routledge.

Glasgow, G. D. (1980). *The Black underclass: Poverty, unemployment, and entrapment of ghetto youth.* London: Jossey-Bass.

Glesne, C. (1997). That rare feeling: Re-presenting research through poetic transcription. *Qualitative Inquiry, 3, 2.*

Gordon, U. J. (2002). *The Black male in White America.* New York. Nova Science.

Gregory, E., Long, S., & Volk, D. (2004). *Many pathways to literacy: Young children learning with sibling, grandparents, peers and communities.* London: RoutledgeFalmer.

Guillory, B. M. (1974). *The Black family: A case for change and survival in White america.* Unpublished doctoral dissertation, Tulane University.

Guion, L. A. (2002). *Triangulation: Establishing the validity of qualitative studies.* Department of Family, Youth and Community Sciences, Florida Cooperative Extension Services, Institute of Food and Agricultural Sciences. University of Florida.

Harris, W. (1992). *Society and culture in the slave south.* New York. Routledge.

Harvey, P. (2005). *Freedom's coming: Religious culture and the shaping of the south from the civil war through the civil rights era.* London: University of North Carolina.

Haskins, J. (1992). *One more river to cross: The stories of twelve Black Americans.* New York. Scholastic.

Henderson, G. (1999).*Our Souls to Keep: Black/White relations in America.* Yarmouth, ME: Intercultural.

Herbers, J. (1973). *The Black dilemma.* New York. John Day.

Herndon, M. K., & Hirt, J. B. (2004). Black students and their families: What leads to success in college. *Journal of Black Studies, 34,* 489-513.

Hill, B. R. (2005). *Informal adaptation among Black families.* D.C: National Urban League.

Ibarra, H., & Lineback, K. (2005). What's your story? *Harvard Business Review,*

Irvin, L. D. (1992). *The unsung heart of black america.* Columbia, MO: University Of Missouri.

Jennings, J. (2003). *Welfare reform and the revitalization of the inner-city neighborhoods.* East Lansing, MI: Michigan State University.

Johnson, B. (2005). *Dubois on reform: Periodical-based leadership for African Americans.* New York. Rowman & Littlefield.

Jones, A. W. (1979). *God in the ghetto.* Elgin, IL: Progressive Baptist Publishing House.

Kain, J. F. (2004). A pioneer's perspective on the spatial mismatch literature. *Urban Studies, 41*,7-32.

Landry, B. (1987). *The new Black middle class.* London: University of California.

Levin, M. J. (1970). *Community control of schools.* Washington., D.C. : The Brookings Institutions.

Lipton, M., & Oakes, J. (1999). *Detracking Schools: Early lessons from the field. Tracked for failure/ tracked for success: An action packet to derail the negative effects of ability grouping.* Task Force on Grouping and Tracking. National Council of Teachers of English. Urbana, IL.

Lipsitz, G. (2006). *The Possessive Investment in Whiteness: How White people profit from identity politics.* Philadelphia, PA: Temple University.

Lockwood, L. (1970). *Conversation with Elbridge Cleaver.* New York. McGraw-Hill.

Lomotey, K. (1990). *Going to school: The African American experience.* Albany, NY: State University of New York.

Lormand, E. (1996). How to be a meaning holist. *The Journal of Philosophy, 93,* 2. Retrieved March 10, 2005,from http://wwpersonal.umich.edu/~lormand/ phil/meaning/holism.htm.

Mandela, N. (1963). *No easy walk to freedom.* Jordan Hill, Oxford: Heinemann Educational Books.

Manen, V. M. (2002). *Writing in the dark: Phenomenological studies in interpretive inquiry.* London: Althouse.

Mariampolski, H. (2001). *Qualitative market research: A comprehensive guide.* Thousand Oaks, CA: Sage.

Martin, E. P., & Martin, J. M. (1995). Social Work and the Black Experience. Washington, D.C. : National Association of Social Workers.

Maxwell, J. (1996). *Hush your mouth!* Terrell, TX: Maxwell.

McGee, L , & Neufeldt, G. H. (1990). *Education of the Africa American adult: An historical overview*. New York. Greenwood.

McGroarty, D. (1996). Bus ride to no-where. *The American Enterprise*, 7, 38-41.

Meares, P. A. (2004). *African American youths: Promoting educational achievement and culturally-sensitive research through the strengths perspective. Reconceptualizing the strengths and common heritage of black families: Practice, research, and policy issues.* Springfield, IL: Charles C. Thomas.

Memmi, A. (2000). *Racism.* London: University of Minnesota.

Miles, R. (1989). *Racism.* New York. Routledge.

Mills, W. C. (1959). *The sociological imagination.* New York. Oxford University.

Mincy, R. (1994). *Nurturing young black males: Challenges to agencies, programs, and social policy.* Washington, D.C.: Urban Institute.

Mitchell, H. H. (1990*). Black preaching: The recovery of a powerful art.* Nashville, TN: Abingdon.

Mithun, J. S. (1973). *Survival as a way of life: Some adaptive mechanisms contributing toward the perpetuation of afro-american culture.* Retrieved March 23, 2005, from http://newfirstsearch oclc.org/WebZ/FSFETCH? Fetchtype=fullrecord: sessionid=sp07sw02 p.15.

Morgan, A. R. (1993). *Slim's table destroys Black male stereotype.* Retrieved September 24, 2005, from http://www.lib.niu.edu/ipo/ii930863.html.

Nelson, J. T. (2005). *Every time i feel the spirit: Religious experience and ritual in an African American church.* New York. New York University.

North Carolina State Department of Public Instruction, Raleigh. Division of Accountability. (2000). *Closing the achievement gap: Views from nine schools.* Retrieved April 21, 2005, from http://www.ncpublicschools.org/closingthegap/nineschools.pdf.

Overacker, I. (1998). *The African American church community in Rochester,* NY: *1900-1940.* Rochester, NY: University of Rochester New York.

Pasquini, M. (2002). *My conclusions: Tracking should be derailed.* Retrieved April 19, 2005, from http://www.ithaca.edu/ jwiggles/t&m/measurement_ practices/tracking/ conclusions.htm.

Patton, Q. M. (2002). *Qualitative research & evaluation methods.* London: Saga.

Pazaratz, D. (2004). An at-risk student and school retaliation. *Journal of School Violence, 3,* 34-61.

Pfautz, W. H. (1963). The new Negro: Emerging american. *Phylon, 24,* 4.

Pinn, B. A. (2002). *The Black in the post-civil rights era.* New York. Orbis.

Quarles, B. (1964). *The Negro in the making of America*. New York. Collier Books.

Ray, R. L. (1971). *The Black college community*. Unpublished doctoral dissertation, University of Massachusetts.

Renninger, A. B., & Steiner, J. N. (1993). *Issues in tracking and ability grouping practices in english language arts classrooms, K-12. Tracked for failure/ tracked for success: An action packet to derail the negative effects of ability grouping.* Task Force on Grouping and Tracking. National Council of Teachers of English. Urbana, IL.

Rocchio, F. V. (2000). *Reel racism: Confronting hollywood's construction of afro-american culture*. Boulder, CO: Westview.

Rodney, H. E., & Tachia, H. R. (1998). *Comprehensive family assessment: Factors impacting violence.* Wilberforce, OH: Central State.

Ronnick, V. M. (2005). *The autobiography of William Sanders Scarborough: An american journey from slavery to scholarship.* Detroit, MI: Wayne State University.

Roscigno, J.V. (1998). Race and the reproduction of educational disadvantage. *Social Forces, 76*, 1033-61.

Rosenberg, B. (1966). *Analyses of contemporary society*. New York. Thomas Y. Crowell.

Rubenstein, H., & Bloch, H. M. (1982). *Things that matter: Influences on helping relationships.* New York, NY: MacMillan.

Schram, H. T. (2003). *Conceptualizing qualitative inquiry: Mindwork for fieldwork in education and the social sciences.* Upper Saddle River, NJ: Merrill/Prentice Hall.

Schwandt, T. (2001). *Dictionary of qualitative inquiry.* Thousand Oaks, CA: Sage.

Scott, M. D. (1997). *Contempt and pity: Social policy and the image of the damaged Black psyche, 1880-1996.* London: University of North Carolina.

Seidman, I. (1998). *Interviewing as qualitative research: A guide for researchers in education and the social sciences.* New York. Teachers College.

Shingles, R. D. (1979). College as a source of Black alienation. *Journal of Black Studies, 9*, 3, 267-289.

Siegle, D. (2004). *A Phenomenological approach to in-depth interviewing.* Retrieved June 6, 2005, from http://www.gifted.uconn.edu/ siegle/research/Qualitative /intervie.htm.

Silverman, D. (1997). *Qualitative research: Theory, method and practice.* London: Sage.

Smith, C. W. (1985). *The church in the life of the Black family.* Valley Forge, PA: Judson.

Snarey, V. W., & Walker, J. R. (2004). *Race-ing moral formation: African American perspectives on care and justice.* New York. Teachers College.

Span, M. C. (2002). I must learn now or not al all: Social and cultural capital in the education initiatives of formerly enslaved African Americans in Mississippi, 1862-1869. *The Journal of African American History.*

Retrieved May 23, 2007, from http://links.jstor.org/sici?sici=1548-

1867%28200221%2987%3C196%3A%22MLNON%3E2.0.CO%3B2-R.

Stanfield, H. J. (1993). Race and ethnicity in research methods. Newbury Park,

CA: Sage.

Staples, R. (1998). Reflections on the Black family future: The implications for

public policy. *The Western Journal of Black Studies,* 12, 19-27.

Stewart, F. C. (1997). *Soul survivors: An African American spirituality.*

Louisville, KY: Westminster John Knox.

Stewart, R. (1991). *African American husbands: A study of black family life.*

Bristol, IN: Wyndham Hall.

Sullivan, L. (1997a). *The impact of homelessness on children.* New York.

Garland.

Sullivan, L. (1997 b). Hip-hop nation: The underdeveloped social capital of Black

urban America. *National Civic Review.* 86, p.235-43.

Swadener, B. B., & Lubeck, S. (1995). *Children and families at promise:*

deconstructing the discourse of risk. Albany, NY: State University of New

York.

Sweeney, B. D. (2007). Give me liberty. *Arts and Activities*, 5, 141.

Tatum, B. D. (1987). *Assimilation blues: Black families in a White community.*

New York. Basic Books.

Thompson, L. H. (1954). *The American Bible Society and the Negro: A study of*

the American Bible Society's bible distribution program among American

Negroes and its effectiveness educationally. Unpublished thesis, Oberlin

Graduate School of Theology at Oberlin, Ohio.

Toliver, S. D. (1982). *The `Black family in slavery, the foundation of afro culture:*

Its importance to member of the slave community. Unpublished

dissertation, University of California at Berkeley.

United States office of Education (1969). *History of schools for the colored*

population. New York. Arno and The New York Times.

Upchurch, C. (1996). *Convicted in the womb.* New York. Bantam Books.

Vivian, T. C. (1970). *Black power and the American myth.* Philadelphia, PA:

Fortress.

Williams, E. L. (1996). *Servants of the people: The 1960's legacy of african-*

american leadership. New York. St. Martin's Griffin.

Wilson, J. W. (1990). *The truly disadvantaged: The inner city, the underclass,*

and public policy. Chicago, IL: University of Chicago.

Young, J. R. (1996). *Antebellum Black Activists: Race, gender, and self.* New

York. Garland.

Youngblood, J. D., & Winn, J. E. (2004). Shout glory: Competing communication

codes experienced by the members of the african-american pentecostal

genuine deliverance holiness church. *Journal of Communication, 54,* 355-

70.

Zuckerman, P. (2000*). Du bois on religion.* New York. Rowman & Littlefield.

113

APPENDIXES

Appendix A

University of West Florida Review Board Approval

University of
West Florida

Office of Research and Graduate Studies
11000 University Parkway
Pensacola, FL 32514-5750

October, 11 2005

Mr. James Richardson
580 Pheasant Court
Pensacola, FL 32514

Dear Mr. Richardson:

The Institutional Review Board (IRB) for Human Research Participant Protection has completed its review of your proposal titled "Beating the Odds: Pedagogy, Praxis and the Life-World of Four Successful African-American Men" as it relates to the protection of human participants used in research, and has granted approval for you to proceed with your study. As a research investigator, please be aware of the following:

• You acknowledge and accept your responsibility for protecting the rights and welfare of human research participants and for complying with all parts of 45 CFR Part 46, the UWF IRB Policy and Procedures, and the decisions of the IRB. You may view these documents on the Office of Research web page at http://www.research.uwf.edu. You acknowledge completion of the IRB ethical training requirements for researchers as attested in the IRB application.

• You will ensure that legally effective informed consent is obtained and documented. If written consent is required, the consent form must be signed by the participant or the participant's legally authorized representative. A copy is to be given to the person signing the form and a copy kept for your file.

• You will promptly report any proposed changes in previously approved human participant research activities to the Office of Research and Graduate Studies. The proposed changes will not be initiated without IRB review and approval, except where necessary to eliminate apparent immediate hazards to the participants.

• **You are responsible for reporting progress of approved research to the Office of Research and Graduate Studies at the end of the project period. Approval for this project is valid for one year. If the data phase of your project continues beyond one year, you must request a renewal by the IRB before approval of the first year lapses. Project Directors of research requiring full committee review should notify the IRB when data collection is completed.**

• You will immediately report to the IRB any injuries or other unanticipated problems involving risks to human participants.

Good luck in your research endeavors. If you have any questions or need assistance, please contact the Office of Research and Graduate Studies at 857-6378.

Sincerely,

Dr. Keith Whinnery, Chair
IRB for Human Research
Participant Protection

Ms. Sandra VanderHeyden
Director of Sponsored Research

cc: Dr. Mary Rogers
      Dr. Richard Podemski

APPENDIX B

Informed Consent Form

Informed Consent Form for Research Conducted by James O. Richardson
Doctoral Student at the University of West Florida

Title of Research: Beating the odds: Pedagogy, praxis and the Life-world of four

African-American men

I Federal and University regulations require researchers to obtain signed consent

for participation in research involving human participants. After reading the

statements in section II through V below, please indicate your consent by signing

and dating this form.

II. Statement of Procedure: Thanks you for your interest in this research
project being conducted by James O. Richardson a doctoral student at the
University of West Florida. The purpose of this study is to generate an
understanding of the life-world and the lived experiences of four African-
American men and or their partners and or their children. Please carefully read the
information below, and if you wish to participate in this study, sign your name
and write the date.

I understand that:

1. All individuals voluntarily participate in this study agree to do several

interviews for generating date.

2. The researcher assured all participants of confidentiality and will change the

names, locations, and any other identifying information that will be referenced in

the study's results.

119

3. The researcher will share the results of this study with my committee members and chairperson and other participants if requested. No participant will be identified in any information shared with the committee members for the purpose of improving future instruction.

4. I may discontinue participation in this study at any time without coercion.

III. Potential Risks of the Study: Benefits of the Study: There are no foreseeable risks to participants in the study.

IV. Potential Benefits of the Study: The results of this study may provide an understanding about the life-world, lived experiences and praxis of four African-American men.

V. Statement of Consent: I certify that I have read and fully understand the Statement of Procedure give above and agree to participate in the research described therein. Permission is given voluntarily and without coercion or undue influence. It is understood that I may discontinue participation at any time.

If you have any questions, please contact James Richardson.

E-mail:	jor2@students.uwf.edu
Phone:	(850) 479-7904
Address:	580 Pheasant ct. Pensacola, Florida 32514